Maybe the worst thing you can do to your children is look at them too closely,
making them the beginning and the end of who you are.

The time will come,

one day,

when they will want to look back at you too.

To find a person, not just a parent.

How do you make sure you'll still be there when they come to find you?

brazen

Praise for *small*:

This book is a rare treasure. Lynch writes of motherhood with fierce intelligence in prose of exquisite beauty. Here is the world – its challenges and wonders, its losses and joys – rendered in such moving detail that I found myself rationing the pages. Reader, beware: you will not want this book to end.
—Emilie Pine

I read it all in one go, heart in my mouth. Such beautiful, beautiful writing about motherhood, parenthood and what it means to bring a child into this world.
—Lucy Caldwell

So good, original, important, moving, funny – quite a feat.
—Bernardine Evaristo

small
on motherhoods
claire lynch

brazen

First published in Great Britain in 2021 by
Brazen, an imprint of
Octopus Publishing Group Ltd
Carmelite House
50 Victoria Embankment
London EC4Y 0DZ
www.octopusbooks.co.uk

An Hachette UK Company
www.hachette.co.uk

First published in paperback in 2022

Text copyright © Claire Lynch 2021, 2022

Distributed in the US by
Hachette Book Group
1290 Avenue of the Americas
4th and 5th Floors
New York, NY 10104

Distributed in Canada by
Canadian Manda Group
664 Annette St.
Toronto, Ontario, Canada M6S 2C8

The right of Claire Lynch to be identified
as the author of this Work has been
asserted by her in accordance with the
Copyright, Designs & Patents Act 1988.

ISBN 978-1-91424-005-8

A CIP catalogue record for this book is
available from the British Library.

Printed and bound in Great Britain

10 9 8 7 6 5 4 3 2 1

This FSC' label means that materials used for
the product have been responsibly sourced

MIX
Paper from
responsible sources
FSC® C104740

The immense success of our life, is I think,
that our treasure is hid away;
or rather in such common things that nothing can touch it.

Virginia Woolf

contents

wonder

You mustn't worry, they don't feel the cold.
Little globes of hope.

Frozen in time.

Like fossils   in reverse.

                    A becoming.

                    ⊛

You've seen it yourself,
a silent movie through the eye of a microscope.
A clear-glass full stop, injected with a comma.

                                        .,

Grey and blue new life.
Human hands out of shot.
                    Human bodies off stage.
Science.
                                        Magic.

So many beginnings in a life.

Two cells meeting is the least of them.

                    ⊛

small

We sit on the floor, side-by-side, and search for him.
The stranger who can make us a family.
Backs to the sofa, legs stretched out. Beth rests the laptop on her
thighs and we scroll through donors.

>Click.

Reject.

>Click.

>>Add to basket.

An online catalogue of implausibly healthy overachievers.
As we browse, I wonder, what makes a man become a
sperm donor?
Bold young men with unshakable self-confidence.
Fathers, so pleased with their own children.
Genetic philanthropists.
Modern-day saints offering help to those in need.
Women limited by biology, circumstance, time.
Men stymied by injury, illness, bad luck.
In lieu of flowers please send donations to the designated womb.

There are no photos.
I didn't want to know his face, to find myself searching out the
shape of his eyes or curve of his jaw in theirs.

>Click.

No.

>Click.

Maybe.

It's like online shopping.
Or online dating.
It's nothing at all like those things.
How can you compute the scale of it?
So easy to make smutty jokes about windowless rooms
and magazines.
So much harder to take in this act of generosity,
so small it can only be seen under a microscope.
So large it sets a whole new world into existence.

And as we sit and browse I ask her,
Would you choose me, as a donor, if I had a profile like this?
—Yes, she says, absolutely.

    —You'd sound like great genetic material,
        on paper.

                 ⊛

At the next appointment the doctor shows us graphs. The things
that didn't work last time.
The treatment options we might consider for the next cycle.
Tweaks and adjustments in drug protocols

                                  in timing.
I like the doctor because I believe in her. I like her small talk too,
the way she poses questions with a polite smile then forgets to
feign interest in the response. I'm convinced by her confidence,
the clarity of a medic's worldview. The way she believes,

unquestionably, that an aching soul can be cured with injectable
hormones or optimal conditions in a Petri dish.
The doctor wears heavy-looking gold earrings and a Chanel scarf.
I watch her mouth moving
and I think,

> I paid for that scarf.

—So we are agreed? The doctor says. An excellent plan of action.
Good, good.

The doctor is looking at me across her desk, smiling, earnest.
Beth is looking at me too, eyebrows raised, waiting for
something, a word maybe.
I nod.
I understand.
I am listening.
And the thought settles in my lap.
New.
Like an honour.
Like a burden.
Like a wish.
Not the first woman, or the only woman, or the last woman, to
know this beginning.
To tell this story.

To get my wife pregnant.

And we have agreed that it would not matter, that love and DNA
are not the same thing.

But still we are drawn to try like this, her body, my egg.
Making a baby who is
hers

          mine

                    ours.

That evening, after dinner, we go back to the online catalogue
and open up the shortlist, the missing piece. Double-checking
the drop-down boxes that invite us to filter by
race,
hair colour,
blood group,
height,
religion,
education,
nationality,
skin tone,
occupation.
There is no category for sense of humour,
or whether he cheats at Monopoly,
or only pretends to understand the offside rule.

We try to read between the lines, search for clues, hints in the
unsaid.
Who, I wonder, picks the sperm donor described as having 'a low
tolerance for sleep deprivation'.
Does that 'cheeky smile' sit on an otherwise repellent face?

Is that 'altruistic nature' code for 'creepily involved in the lives of others?'

We compare and contrast, we deliberate and gamble, try, somehow, to take into account a stranger's proficiency at the piano or whether it is more challenging to have an allergy to wheat or pollen.

Or.

There is another beginning.

A different city. Beth. Me. Ourselves and not. Just students. Knowing, or fearing, that we were falling in love. Trying to avoid each other, trying not to betray the relationships we were in. All the same, in the last week of term, she arrived at my front door wearing broken fairy wings and tinsel in her hair, the laziest of Christmas party costumes,

and kissed me.

And I spent my days in the library, sometimes reading the books I needed for my thesis, mostly reading the books I didn't. Thinking of her, three streets away, in her lab, high above the city. In the evenings she would listen, patiently, to the dull trouble I was having with a footnote.

I would try, and fail, to understand her experiments.

The mysteries of molecular dynamics.

                    Atoms. Molecules. Simulations.

For months I thought that the protein she was studying sounded romantic. Poor Stargazin mice, named for the genetic mutation

that fixes their heads back, forcing their sights to the stars.
Later, we moved to London, a carload of possessions, mostly
books.
To a flat that was really a room, close to the tube station, a dry-
cleaners and an Iranian supermarket with windows full of real
goldfish at Persian New Year. On the first morning we ate our
breakfast with wooden spoons because we couldn't find cutlery.

Our baby began then too. On all those days. In all those places.

◉

In the waiting room of the fertility clinic, Beth and I sit among
strangers, bound by a shared dilemma: the thing we want most is
the thing we cannot have.
On the wall next to the coffee machine is a gallery of baby
photos, sent to the clinic by previous patients. A display of tiny
fists and huge eyes. Endorsements from satisfied customers.
Some of us will leave here with what we came for. Some of us will
simply learn to avoid Regent's Park tube station.

Find another book shop.
Another favourite cafe.

◉

The human egg is the largest cell in the body. Round and
glowing, in biology textbooks and on fertility websites.

small

Welcoming. Electric. Like planets far away from here.
In one of the clinic's glossy leaflets I read that one hundred
human eggs set side-by-side would measure just over a
centimetre. I doodle them in the margin, one hundred tiny dots
of biro. One hundred possible babies.

....
....
....
....

I notice that the woman sitting by the door hasn't turned the
page of her book in twenty minutes. The couple sitting opposite
us grip hands, watch the muted news channel without blinking.
By the window, a woman talks loudly on her phone, asks her PA
to reschedule this afternoon's meeting. She isn't talking to any of
us but we all understand what she is saying. She is an important,
professional woman, she doesn't need a baby really, she is fine.
        Absolutely fine.
Some people fiddle with their phones, some fill in forms, some
sip coffee (decaffeinated) from takeaway cups.
Nobody looks at the wall of baby pictures.

She was born three years before me, the first IVF baby.
Conceived, not in a test tube, but in the clear shallow pool of a
Petri dish. I remember the pictures of her on the news a few years
ago, celebrating her fortieth birthday. When she was born, along

with all the pink congratulations cards, her parents received
hate mail. Sloppy letters splashed with red ink, plastic foetuses
wrapped in cotton wool, addressed to 'The Test Tube Baby,
Bristol'. I search for images of her online and see her smiling face,
over and over on the screen of my phone. Louise Brown, mother-
of-two, holding the incubating jar she began in. They keep
the jar in a museum now, a relic of scientific hope and human
accomplishment, that looks, for all the world, like a
Pyrex cooking dish.

Fertility clinics, like the mafia, have very few exit strategies. For
those who don't reach the happy ending of a baby there's still an
ending, one way or another.
Maybe your money runs out, or your eggs, or your sanity.

I can hardly bear to think about the beginning.
How naive we were, how little we understood.

We kept the drugs schedule on the fridge,
columns for injections,

                    tablets,
                    vitamins,
                    suppositories.

                    Rows for dates, scans, procedures.
A little heart doodled next to the test date.
The irony of it all too obvious, like a sticker chart you would

make for a toddler potty training, or to remind children to feed
the guinea pig. After each embryo transfer the clinic would give
us a scan picture and we'd add that to the fridge too. Pinning it
at eye level with a magnet of the Sydney Opera House. A scan
picture, just like those you have seen online, but much, much
smaller. No tiny head, no arms and legs. Just the black and grey
of cells and womb, a star of white light, the dot we called our
baby. For two weeks we would look at it each time we passed
through the kitchen. Making a wish as we loaded the dishwasher.
Whispering a prayer when we took out the bins. Looking at
each pixel of the picture as if you could see it changing. See it
becoming real.

Each failed attempt was a lesson in reality, another dent in our
hope. I spent hours then, lurking on online forums, scouring the
potted biographies of strangers for tips and clues. Eat pineapple
core, try acupuncture, buy flax seed. Women still trying after ten,
eleven, twelve cycles of unsuccessful treatment. A commitment.
An addiction.

I studied the signatures on their profiles, the winged angel emojis
and code words. TTC and FET and BFN. Women who lived
in a parallel universe of what might have been. Their longed-for
children who should have been in school now, the babies who
never were, who might have been big enough to ride a bike this
summer. At first I only read threads on symptoms and treatment,
searching for insider information, some vital detail we might

have missed. In time I read the forums as a sort of punishment, seeking out stories of other people's success so I could wallow in the unfairness of it all. How dare these strangers be so happy? At some stage, I began to navigate to the threads called 'Letting Go' or 'Moving On'. Daring myself to read stories about finding some other way to live. Fertility forums are full of these, brave and thoughtful stories of people freeing themselves at last. Not easily, and not without scars, but with dignity, with resolve. And each time, amid all the good sense, the comforting solidarity, I will find it, the post that undermines it all. The person who insists on saying, never give up, keep on trying. You never know when your time will come. And so people are trapped in limbo. Pulled one way by logic and evidence, pulled the other by the unrelenting force of hopefulness. Many IVF patients who are advised to stop treatment carry on anyway, because it's a little less painful to keep going than to stop.

Are we those people now? Storm-blown seabirds, clinging to our plan. So lost in our desire to become parents that we barely see the process we're caught up in. Taking for granted all the burdens, seeing the physical strains as just necessary obstacles along the course. There is something delusional about it, the repetition. Another final attempt. Sitting in the room of strangers, again. Waiting, hoping, drinking the coffee that might be tea, not looking at the pictures of babies that aren't ours. In one way IVF is a simple equation.

A question of numbers.

small

The doctors talk about likelihoods, percentages, averages.
As if it is merely a question of making an accurate calculation.
As if it isn't, in the end, just a matter of luck.

                                        A game of chance.

To maximize the number of eggs I can produce I'm prescribed
daily injections and several types of tablet. As the weeks pass I
travel back and forth to the clinic to have my ovaries scanned
and follicles measured, and by the day of the egg collection I
can barely walk. My swollen ovaries press into my other organs,
I am bloated, uncomfortable and I am really, really, hungry.
Glossy magazine articles that suggest high-flying career women
might nip out on a lunch break to freeze their eggs omit these
details. On the ward the nurse hands me a surgical gown and
blue plastic shower caps to wear over my feet.
—Remove your underwear, please. She says. Hop up here on the
        bed and put your legs in the stirrups.
Forget your lifetime of birds and bees. Storks and honeymoons.
None of it prepared you for this.

I divert all my attention to looking at the clock,
and then the lights,
and then the air conditioning unit.

I look at the clock again,
and the ceiling,
and the air conditioning unit once more,

and the lights again.

Because, in truth, there is nothing more to do here than survive
the minutes.

The nurse makes small talk about the traffic in central London
and as she moves on to talking about the congestion charge
she arranges stainless-steel instruments, fiddling with her
latex gloves.

I look at the ceiling light again.

Eventually, the gynaecologist comes in, adjusts her seat at the
end of the bed between my swinging ankles, making (mercifully
brief) small talk.

                              Finally, the anaesthetist.

A roomful of strangers.

He takes my hand, warns me of the sharp scratch. I go along with
the fiction and he slides the needle into the back of my left hand,
an oxygen mask over my face, cold sleep running up my arm and
all over me.
Something is given now,
something taken.
Flat on my back, the doctors in their gowns and masks,

small

bringing them forth.
A small birth.

Swimming up from sedation in the recovery room the nurse
gives me tea and biscuits, compensation for my knickerless work.
I hold the plastic cup in two hands, propped up in the bed as
the embryologist appears, all clipboards and confidence. He
is extremely tall, capable, surely, of peering over the top of the
curtained cubicles.

The tall embryologist delivers the news in the measured tone of a
man who has never bought an electrical appliance without doing
considerable consumer research first.

—Twenty-two eggs have been collected, he says, and the sperm
        sample looks excellent.

How odd it is, to feel grateful that a man you haven't met has
produced exemplary sperm.

How foolish, to feel proud of your own body for generating cells,
as if you have done it by force of your own will.

The nurse has put sugar in my tea, to speed up my recovery, to see
me on my way.

                                    It is horrible. I drink it all.

®

We drive home, empty of eggs, full of hope.

16

Try to sleep, Beth says,
we'll be there soon.

And as she takes us out of the city I dream through the dregs of
the anaesthetic, thinking of my parents' wedding photographs.
His flared trousers, her pink cheeks. My mother, nobody's
mother then, only eighteen. Sandwiches and sausage rolls at the
reception. As a child I was fascinated by my absence from it all.
The impossibility of my parents existing before me.
They didn't need all of this. No injections, no scans, no private
clinics. They played their parts flawlessly. The wedding day, the
deposit put down on the house, a girl, a boy, three years apart
almost to the day.

Clockwork.

When I open my eyes we are slipping along a flyover, the western
edges of the city spread out below us, advertising boards as tall as
houses, tower blocks and car showrooms. I look down over the city,
see how full it is, how busy, and try to focus on all that we have left
behind there. The small circle of the Petri dish, the smaller circles
of embryos inside them. And I feel a sort of duty, to hold them in
my thoughts, as if I have some connection, some power over them.
As if I can will the eggs to survive, to fertilize, to grow. But I'm
too tired, the anaesthetic not quite shaken off. My mind slips and
stumbles through strange connections. When I close my eyes again
I remember a different egg altogether, the boiled egg my father
made me for breakfast the day my brother was born.

small

—The egg is a treat, he said. A special breakfast to celebrate the
    new baby.
I wouldn't eat it and there wasn't time to argue. We had to walk
across town for visiting hours, one of his strides to three of mine,
an ache in my shoulder from reaching up to keep my small hand
in his. Swept up and along from dawdling steps or pavement
distractions, cracked paving slabs and dropped coins. This is the
egg I grew from, my first memory. The egg that sat on the kitchen
table, slowly cooling, shell uncracked, as I met my new baby
brother for the first time. No longer hungry, but very sticky, from
the only breakfast my father could improvise from the corner
shop by the hospital.
I was three and I understood everything; *babies are as easily
acquired as ice lollies.*

print

To find out if she was pregnant, an Ancient Egyptian woman would urinate into two bags of grain.

If the wheat sprouted, she was having a girl, if the barley grew, a boy.

No sprouts of life in the grain meant no sprouts of life in the woman.

By the early twentieth century, scientists had learned that injecting the urine of a pregnant woman into a rabbit would cause the animal to ovulate. The trouble for the rabbit, of course, was that the creature had to be dissected before anyone could confirm this had happened.

Frogs were found to be a little more convenient. Until the 1960s countless African clawed frogs responded to their injections of pregnant women's piss by spontaneously producing eggs. Unlike the godforsaken rabbits, frogs could be used as a hopping pregnancy test several times over.

It's been two weeks since the embryo transfer, two weeks since the tall embryologist carefully carried our little ball of cells from the lab to Beth's body. Two weeks of wondering, two weeks of living alongside the possibility of it all. Two weeks since Beth lay back on that same bed in the same clinic, the spaces between us big and small. My cells binding onto hers.

Beth spreads out the pregnancy test leaflet on the edge of the bathroom sink and reads the instructions. The optimal number of seconds to pee on a stick. The choice to dip or catch the flow

mid-stream. Easier to catch a frog.
I wait outside the bathroom door, telling myself quiet lies.
       Things will be ok.
              Whatever happens next.
Because so many things will happen in the world in the next
three minutes. Bigger things than two women, standing either
side of a bathroom door in their small house and small lives.
This is only three minutes of waiting.
       Which follows two weeks of waiting.
           Which follows a month of waiting.
               Which follows all these years of waiting.
All the years of wanting.

Three minutes of waiting for a blue line to appear,

                        or not.
Watching the seconds flick over on my phone's stopwatch.
We've coped before, we tell each other.
We know what to do next.
Some crying together.
Some rage at the injustice of it all.
Some crying alone.
A long walk, a call to the clinic to start again.
               Unless.
Perhaps this time is different from the others.
The thought, an exquisite little torture.
Maybe, this is the time?
But there's a long way to go, other snares and traps.

The last minute.

    The last thirty seconds.

These are the places where your life changes forever.

Sitting on the landing carpet.

Picking dried toothpaste from the edge of the sink.

Waiting for the seconds to pass.

And perhaps it goes without saying, that the moment is not quite as I had always imagined. That in a lifetime of watching pregnancy test cliffhangers in movies and soap operas I had never seen a woman on both sides of the bathroom door. Still, I had imagined it, one way or another, I had been trained all my life to treat motherhood as an inevitability. Misled to believe any alternative was either an eccentricity or tragedy.

Every woman has stories like these.

The blessed assumption that mothers and women are the same thing.

My first time was in a supermarket.

I was twenty, home from university for the summer and drawn to 'Staff Wanted' signs. The job looked easy enough, a few hours a day behind the counter at the back of the supermarket where they developed photographs. Pictures of babies in baths, children standing by the front door on the first day of school. Five days a week spent looking into the lives of strangers. Weddings and caravan holidays.

Pictures of the cat or the car to use up the last of the film.

small

When I asked the manager for an application form she was
annoyed at the interruption.
—Tell me about yourself first, do you have any children?
　　　　And I laughed.
　　　　　　　And left.
　　　　　　　　　Then went home to tell my mother the joke.
Can you believe it? I said. What a question. She didn't ask if I
could use the till or speak to customers. Who has kids at my age?
—My mum had me at that age, my mother said. And I had you.

These are the available options, a humming background
presumption, that you can either be a mother or a mother-
in-waiting. Present or future tense. Unsubtle queries in job
interviews. Pointed hints from a mother-in-law. Questions of
when, not if, you will transform. Pass from this life to your true
vocation. I tell my friends about this memory, the job that I never
applied for, and we laugh, not at the lazy expectation that all
women must want to be mothers, but at the fact we had forgotten
that you once had to wait for photos to be developed. We are all
appalled that we used to live with this inconvenience. This test
of patience. Imagine it, not knowing what was hidden inside the
camera for weeks or months. Those cameras are in a museum
now, we say, next to the blacksmiths and VHS machines.
We're almost too busy laughing to hear Jen say,
—People do stop asking.
　　　　—Eventually.

And of course there is one way to sidestep it, to confound
the expectations.
Two bodies that can't make a baby raise different assumptions,
different tactless questions.

Beth and I are used to the questions now.
The just-curious questions. The personal questions. The practical
and intrusive ones.
—How much will it cost? Or, have you really thought it all
through?
—How, if you don't mind me asking, will you actually do it?
People ask this, at parties, standing by the fridge, drinking wine
from plastic cups, a handful of crisps.
There is no privacy when you have to make your baby by
committee.

    Doctors, nurses, lab technicians.

    One donor.

    Two mothers.

And sometimes I am glad to be asked. It is tempting, to talk the
baby into being.

                    And sometimes it is another injury,
to have another piece of our intimacy made public.
No privilege of a happy accident.
No seaside postcard punchline: *at least you had fun trying.*

And we have talked and talked and talked between ourselves.
About how and when and why, but it isn't enough, we have to

25

talk in front of someone else. Before starting treatment the
fertility clinic requires patients to attend mandatory counselling
sessions. It is exposing, insulting, having to explain our desires to
others. Having to perform our suitability as parents.
Couples who are able to make a baby with their own bodies
don't have to explain their motivations to a frizzy-haired
woman. They don't have to prove themselves ready or worthy
or suitable.
It takes me years to understand that the counselling isn't about
allowing us to have a baby.

It's to prepare us for what will happen if we can't.

The counsellor's office is large and white.
Big sash windows looking out over the street.
She invites us to sit in low chairs,
places a box of tissues on the glass coffee table between us.
—So tell me, she says, why do you want to have a baby?
And it is all too tempting to say,
—Because we're hoping to breed a rebel army to overthrow
        capitalism.
—Because we don't like cats.
—Because there's nothing good on television these days.

But we don't.

That morning, I'd spent two hours worrying about what to wear.
Because I thought we should dress like parents.
Because I thought we shouldn't look too gay.

The counsellor asks us about our childhoods.

Beth talks about growing up by the sea.

I concede a story about having pet rabbits.

—And what story will you tell the baby, the counsellor asks,
about how they were made?

She shows us picture books, cartoon mothers talking to their
cartoon children about eggs and seeds and the kind man and the
clever doctors. They will have this at least, I think, this gift of an
origin story that is all about how much they were wanted and not
at all about their parents having sex.

That is something.

She asks how we will explain how we made our family to our
employers, our neighbours, the curious postman. She asks what
the baby will call us. How we will handle prejudice and hurtful
misunderstandings? How we will cope?

And we say,

—Because we have to.

—Because we love the baby already.

For weeks, I ask myself the counsellor's question. As I wait for the
train. As I stand in the shower. Why *do* I want to have a baby?

All the things I could do instead; drive a tidy car and wear dry-
clean-only clothes, go on city breaks and have expensive haircuts.

I *could* train for marathons.

I *could* adopt a dog.

I could stay out late and sleep in at weekends. Isn't that what
parenting will mean, a giving up of my own plans, my own

freedoms? Somewhere along the way I worry I've picked up the wrong idea, that a good mother is an invisible one. Absorbed the pernicious myth that the ideal mother is a sort of child's personal assistant, anticipating all their needs, leaving no trace of effort. There are so many other women to be.

> The woman who is the best aunt in the whole world.
> The woman who will not let herself cry in the toilets when a colleague announces she is pregnant, again.
> The woman who grows older, stronger, joins a book group and learns Italian.
> The woman who says, my students are my children really, when they are no such thing.

In the last session, the counsellor walks over to her desk and takes out two tubes, woven in blue and white paper.

—They're called Chinese finger traps, she tells us.

> —Place an index finger in each end. Now, take them out.

When I pull my hands apart the tube tightens and grips my fingers. The harder I pull, the tighter it holds.

—There's a lesson in this, the counsellor says.

—Is it, don't put your fingers in something called a finger trap?
> I ask her.

The counsellor is tired.

She folds her hands in her lap and looks at me.

—You need to understand, she says quietly, there are other ways
> to nurture.

> **—Having a baby isn't the only way.**

◉

But all of that was so long ago, so far away from this moment. All of those questions and conversations, injections and scans that led to this. Three minutes of waiting to see if your life has changed.

Whether or not the treatment has worked, it has already changed us. This possible baby already staking its claim on our lives, displacing, at last, the imaginary one who has grown quietly in the shadows over all these years of waiting. I would know him anywhere, the small boy with dark curly hair. A dream child. A work of my imagination, a comfort and a cancer. The shadow baby has sat behind us on each drive to the clinic. He's waited at the airport every time we've tried to go away to forget about him. He's always at family parties or crawling at the feet of friends when they announce the news of another pregnancy. I know other people have them too. I've seen a shadow baby on a woman's lap when her friends smirk knowingly as she orders an orange juice instead of a glass of wine. When conversations are swiftly changed about spare bedrooms going to waste, or biological clocks ticking, you can see them, snuggled in the crook of an elbow, resting on a hip.

Beth goes back into the bathroom, picks up the test from the edge of the sink. Its window the size of a fingernail,

small

the view,
two
life-
changing
parallel   lines.

voice

I know I shouldn't be here.

    Not yet.

Lurking in the baby clothes aisle of the supermarket, rifling through the envelope-necked vests. Touching the tiny sleeves that fold over into mittens. All of the things I never allowed myself to do, before.   It is self-harm.

Newborn baby clothes are designed to make people feel this way. Designed to make adults protect, hold gently. The fabrics, soft fleece, plump velour, pure cotton. All white and cream and pastel pink and blue. Teddy bears and ducklings, giraffes and elephants with rounded features and softened feet. Everything muffled and padded to ease the shock of arriving into a hard world.

I know what she is going to say before I answer.

Something in the ringtone sees me.

Catches me in the act.

Which is nonsense.

Which is true.

I swipe the screen to answer Beth's call and she doesn't say hello, just:

—**I need you to come home,**

    now.

I run to the car,

as if a few minutes will make a difference.

I drive too fast.

small

I run from the car and through the front door knowing, already.
When I ask her if it is over...   she nods.

Later, I drive back to the supermarket
       to buy pizza,
       ice cream,

                      sanitary towels.

I like supermarkets at night, the strip lighting lowered, the aisles
semi-deserted like streets on Christmas Day. The obliging smiles
and nods between strangers. We all have our reasons for being
here so late.
Shift work,
insomnia,
loneliness,
other.

Tonight, it is hard to know where it would be worse to be. At
home, where we would be together, but with nobody between
us to temper our sadness. No obligation to behave as though
everything is fine. Or here, on my own, and not, surrounded by
people working, shopping, wandering. In the supermarket I keep
walking, find the things we need, pay for them, I talk normally to
the person on the checkout. I answer her questions about why I
don't have a loyalty card, agree to pick up a leaflet on my way out.
And I do it too, take the leaflet from the Perspex stand, fold it
into my back pocket.

Because I said I would.
Because I know she is still watching me. What else could I
have done? Worn a sign around my neck that reads: my heart is
broken, please do not speak to me. I am still in the same clothes.
It has only been a few hours. The small bewildering distance. Just
seconds between contentment and misery. A few hours since I
stood in the same shop and let a little girl's name bounce around
the edges of my brain.

In the darkness of the supermarket car park I fold my scarf onto
the steering wheel and howl into it.
A noise I didn't know I could make,
and tell myself something I know to be true.
When unbearable things happen, the breakfast dishes still need
to be washed.
The bedsheets still need to be changed.
The bins taken out.
The plants watered.
The lights turned on.

I decide there, in the car park of a supermarket, that I will
postpone this grief.
Compress it.
Turn it down.
I will bring the shopping home.
Turn the oven on.

small

Beth has a hot bath, a glass of wine.
We endure the night.
When the sound of bin lorries on the street marks the start of the
morning I force myself into the shower and then to my desk.
I call the doctor and hear my voice say,
—Hello. *My wife is having a miscarriage.*

On the way to the clinic we plan our escape. We could go to
America, to New York maybe, drink cocktails in loft apartments
and lose ourselves on long straight streets.
Or somewhere beautiful, beside a lake, or with a view of the sea.
Anywhere but here. Anywhere but in these minds.
When the nurse calls that afternoon with the blood test results
we are told to wait.
—Hard to say for sure, she says.
        Early days.
Bed rest. Patience. Positive thinking.
Wait and see.
We are lost in grief. We are immune to more pain.
We are resolved to try again. We are ready to give up.

                                                Wait and see.

Try to rest in all this unknowing.

And the bleeding stops.

I learn not to ask how she is feeling.
She is feeling everything.

She feels twinges and pains that might be nothing and
might not.
She feels sick,   and then not.
Tired,   and then not.
Sick again.
            Tired again.
                        Bruised.
She feels her cells. She feels the baby's cells. Begs them.

                                              Grow.

Stay.
I move for the both of us.
Running.
Fields and streets.
Running through the park with the kidney-shaped duck pond
and a hut that sells ice creams in the summer.
Running past the park gates where the men and women stand
with their leaflets,
            rosary beads, plastic foetuses.
Shouting at women.
            Shouting at the women at the bus stop too, just in case
                        they need to hear it.
                        Shouting their catchphrase. Their threat.
                        Life begins at conception.
The fabulous old woman I once saw stop in front of the
ringleader to say,
—You've got that wrong for a start love, life begins at forty.

small

A week later we drive into the city. The same waiting room.
The same coffee and magazines.
Waiting for a reprieve, one way or another.
Only some of us will leave here with what we came for.
In the ultrasound room I sit on one side of the curtain with the
nurse as Beth undresses behind it.
The scan begins and the nurse turns to me, asks if I can see
anything.
So I look, at the black screen beside Beth's bed, at the universe
inside her.
Absurdly under-qualified.
And I think then, of course this is how it ends.

                                                            Again.

Beth looks at me, waits for my answer.
Is this what they do? Ask the partner to deliver the bad news.
To soften the blow, or make it real.
—I'm not sure, I say. Two small black shapes?
—That's right, says the nurse. There are two babies.
        —What kind of car do you have?

sounds

Each Friday morning an email arrives with an update on the babies' development. I read the instalments as if they are envoys from the womb rather than the National Health Service, and report the latest progress. Now the nostrils are starting to form.

Now the kidneys.

Now the fingernails.

Each message includes a picture, computer-generated balls of cells that grow into digital foetuses. Balloon wombs in luncheon-meat pink.

At work, I read the emails over and over, thinking about the three of them going about their day. Beth at her desk or in meetings. The babies floating through it all, eavesdropping. Discussions about budgets and marketing strategies muffled and distorted in their gills. The emails are detailed, practical. And then, like a metaphysical poem, the message that tells me, if there's a girl in there, she will be born with all of her eggs already in place, waiting to mature as she grows. I try to think of that part of myself, an unimaginably small Russian Doll, not just within my mother but also my grandmother. These babies are not growing inside my body now, but I have held them there, at least in part, all my life.

Some women say they don't feel pregnant, believe it even, until they see the pictures.

small

The sounds we cannot hear, bouncing waves off bone and water
to sketch two tiny heads.

    The buds that will be limbs.

The sounds we can, the technician cooing and humming as she
measures.

    Head to rump.

    Their heartbeats.

                      Surprisingly loud.

                      Irrefutable.

Machines invented to detect invisible flaws in the sides of ships.

Echoes that paint pictures in black and white.

Sweet progress, these ultrasounds.

I look up their forebears.

Nineteenth-century wax models, intricate embryo sculptures
mounted on wooden plinths.

Worse still, eighteenth-century engravings,

a baby tightly curled in on itself, the mother sliced at the thigh as
if she were a leg of beef.

—Some people have the scan pictures made into key rings, the
      nurse tells us.

    —Or cushions.

They should do it with photos of the parents, I think.

Before and after pictures. Eyes wide, hair on end.

We were never the same again.

—These ones are complimentary, she says, handing me the print-
      outs,

burnished copper embryos with perfect noses and folded ears.

Bodies curved and coy like rare deep-sea creatures.

For the next scan we are sent to the hospital on the outskirts of town, past the station and the racecourse. We follow the signs, up to the second floor, through the double doors and past the lift to the children's ward and antenatal unit, one corridor for every tense of baby.

Walls plastered with laminated orders.

> DO NOT TAKE PICTURES.
> TURN OFF YOUR MOBILE PHONE.
> ALL PATIENTS MUST REPORT TO RECEPTION.
> YOUR NOTES ARE YOUR RESPONSIBILITY.
> *An inhospitable hospital.*

But, from inside her body, a welcoming wave.
Twelve weeks' growth. Round bellies and stretching arms.
> **They've grown.**

At home that evening we use the measuring tape from my sewing box to see their size for ourselves. Bodies the width of my palm. We encourage them. Grow more, keep growing. Prize marrows. We Google the words in the notes we don't understand. And we pause at the doctor's red asterisk, her note in the margin.
*Same-sex parents.

At fifteen weeks, the email tells me, our babies are beautiful monsters. Bodies coated in a layer of soft hair, the curls of

small

eyelashes tickling their cheeks. At sixteen weeks, their abstract
features become realist portraits. Eyes and ears settling in place.
At twenty, the nurse asks,
—Do you want to know what colour to paint the nursery?

We have no interest in blue and pink, but we do want to know
them better,
                    our little strangers.

And so, she lets the word baby evaporate and in its place says,
—This little girl is doing just fine over here,
and then,
sliding the scanner across the new arc of Beth's belly,
—so is her sister.

New words in our mouths.

Daughters.

minds

The antenatal classes take place in a community hall, every Tuesday evening for six weeks.

At one end of the hall is a pool table with a plywood cover to stop people picking at the felt.
At the other, a stage, framed with a display of pottery faces, presumably made by children.
A hall of forgotten things from childhood, Brownies, jumble sales and tap-dancing classes.

We arrive early for the first session, nervous, excited to meet the other new parents-in-waiting. Plastic chairs have been thoughtfully arranged in a semi-circle to allow for an unrestricted view of the bug-eyed plate-faces. Our teacher is setting up her flip chart and greets us, not with a welcome, but an apology.
—I'm just going to say sorry from the start, she blurts. I'm bound to say the wrong thing, you know, with the language, about all of this.
She gestures vaguely between our midriffs, indicating, it seems, that she is aware that we have the same genitals, and turns back to her flip chart.
It is only several hours later that it occurs to me that this might have been our cue to ask for a refund and leave without further insult or expense.

                              Instead, we take a seat.

Our guide to all things childbirth, Paula, wears the same wide-fit sandals and blouse each week as if it were a uniform. She has two grown-up children of her own and it is clear she will never be as happy again as she was when they were babies.

It is equally clear that she doesn't know what to do with me.

In fact, she suggests, it might be better if I sit the first activity out.

—It can get really physical, she warns.

She wouldn't want me to get hurt.

At this unexpected announcement the men in the group start to give each other sideways glances. At worst they thought they might have to watch a birth video; nobody said anything about bare-knuckle fighting. Lacking an alternative, I stride towards the circle, adopting a gait which suggests surprising physical strength, or at least hints, I hope, at a woman who might have been inter-county judo champion in her youth.

Following her directions, the dads-to-be and I link arms and move slowly outwards to make the circle larger, signifying, as it turns out, the dilation of the cervix. Paula encourages us to tussle a little bit, she wants us to demonstrate how reluctant the cervix is to do its duty. Two of the men offer a half-hearted push and shove. Others manage a foot shuffle or a sheepish tug of an arm. The result is a sort of absurd folk dance as the circle gets smaller and larger and smaller again.

Our wives look on, visibly alarmed. Cervical dilation already sounded implausible and this exercise isn't convincing them otherwise.

From her station at the flip chart Paula tells us about the

miraculous transition from a hole the size of a penny to one the size of a bagel, which is not in any way reassuring. Meanwhile, back in the cervix chorus line, the dads and I are getting into our stride. Adding a few kicks to our routine until we are told to sit down.

At some stage, presumably the 1970s, it was agreed that antenatal matters would best be demonstrated through the medium of knitting. And so, Paula shows us an impressive collection of knitted breasts, placentas, umbilical cords and various other reproductive organ tea cosies. In the second week of the course she produces a tableau of little plastic doctors and nurses to indicate how many people might be in attendance at a hospital birth. Her most compelling visual aids, however, are the laminated pictures of infant skin ailments, many of which, it transpires, are case studies drawn from her own offspring. Paula asks us to gather around the table on which she has spread images of severe baby acne, some raw flaky eczema, swollen baby scrotums, and the crusty mouth sores of impetigo. We are all surprised to learn that we are about to partake in a game.
—You have to read the description of symptoms on these, Paula explains, gleefully handing out more laminated cards.
—Now, you have to match them to the pictures.

Thus we pass half an hour playing spot the nappy rash and hunt the ringworm.

small

®

She labours the point, the class instructor.
  Signs of labour.
  Stages of labour.
    Worksheets.
    Diagrams.
            Plastic babies.
Now she wants a division of labour:
mums to the front of the room, dads to the back,
she instructs with a clammy clap of her hands.

            The middle of the room is mine.
            Paused in no-woman's land,
I look at Beth.
She is embarrassed for me and angry, her right hand on
our bump.
I send the three of them a smile, find a seat at the back among the
cervix chorus line and pick up the marker pen.
                    A labour of love.

Because I don't want to be a dad.

I don't go to the classes for an apprenticeship in fatherhood.

I could stop going, they're not compulsory.
I could opt out of this weekly ordeal.

· I could sit at home and watch YouTube videos about contractions without anyone insulting me.

Each week I wonder why I don't.

I keep going to the classes because Beth wants me to, because she needs to be anchored to other people, she wants a community. She wants to talk to other people living through this right now, to the people lying awake. Veins rushing with anticipation. Full of what is to come.
The least I can do is sit by her side.
And aren't the classes teaching me everything I need to know?

That none of this will be easy.
That my motherhood will make some people uncomfortable.
That people will make me feel lost here, if I let them.
This is my education in forbearance.

    In biting my lip.

        In rising above.

            In playing the compromise.
Surely all parents need that.

And I understand at last, the point of the classes isn't just to give us some practical tips, it's an exercise in denial and displacement. A place to turn our eagerness, our naivety, into small pragmatisms.
We talk, endlessly, about placing the baby at the foot of the cot.
We discuss, at length, the pros and cons of swaddling.

small

All, it seems, to avoid thinking about the sheer overwhelming
size of it all.

There are no classes on how to make sure your child is happy
without being selfish, no group discussions on how to teach them
to be brave without being reckless. I'm almost sure I can figure
out how the bottle sterilizer works by myself, but what I really
want, and what all of us sitting in the circle of plastic chairs need,
is for someone to tell us *how on earth we are supposed to help new
people live in the world.*

There are so many things I don't know.
I don't know what it is like to have people ask when I am due or
offer me a seat on the bus.
I don't know the intrusion of a stranger reaching out to touch me
or the burden of their first assumptions and advice.
I don't know what it feels like to have a baby move or stretch
inside my body.
I don't know what it is like to give birth.
I don't know how tiring it is, or how frightening, or how
wonderful.
But my wife knows these things, or will know them all soon
enough, and I worry that it might draw a line between us.
The things we can and cannot share.
—It will cut the other way too, Beth reminds me,
          it's you they'll look like.
She opens the scan pictures on her phone and laughs, see, she

already has your nose. It is true, poor thing. We both need it, this
compromise of biology that binds us all together. A safety net
for the dead-eyed nights we have been warned of, removing the
sinful possibility of anyone screaming,
—She's your baby...

⊛

Each class, after the tea break, the dads and I are sent to the far
corner of the hall so our wives can discuss piles and placentas
without upsetting us. We are given worksheets designed to coax
us into parental responsibility. So little is expected of these men.
Of us.
This week Paula provides lists of domestic chores so that we can
familiarize ourselves with housework. We are supposed to tick
jobs we will generously demean ourselves to do within the initial
hours after our partners give birth.

Some light vacuuming while her stitches heal, perhaps.

Warming up a frozen pizza while the epidural wears off.
Aziz tries to explain that he does all the ironing in their house.
Simon tells us he has always done the cooking.

These men are vulnerable and thoughtful. They are desperate to
understand what their wives' bodies are going through. They are
all capable of switching on the oven.
When Paula walks away, back to the women's group, we lean
back in our plastic chairs and change the subject. Sometimes the
men talk unguardedly, they tell morality tales, warnings from

other menfolk we might all learn from. Simon tells us about his friend who worked away a lot, good money, long hours. The little boy who wouldn't come to him, didn't recognize him even. They pull at threads, stories of their own fathers. Men to respect but not copy. The dad who would not wrap his arms around his grown-up son, in grief, or celebration. A firm handshake the limit of their contact and comfort. The dad who believed in old-fashioned discipline for boys. End it with you, we agree. Don't pass it on.

Tonight, in our annex by the pool table, the future dads and I have been asked to produce a spider diagram of our fears and worries about becoming 'fathers'. Ben is worried about not getting enough sleep. Simon admits he is dreading all the blood. Can't stand it. Never could. They are all very worried about parking arrangements at the hospital. I feel like a spy in the camp when they talk like this, anxious that I might be curbing them, but suspecting that the opposite is true, that somehow I am diffusing it just a little. Permitting something more.
—I mean, says Aziz, you all know what I'm worried about.
And he raises his eyebrows, leaving his darkest fear unspoken.
It seems to be in deference to me that he doesn't just write WILL I EVER HAVE SEX AGAIN? in red letters across our flip chart paper.
We sit in manly silence for a few moments contemplating this fate until Ben says,
—I'm worried about something going wrong.

That Sunday I find a dead mouse outside the back door and, if it wasn't dead already, I would want to kill it. I hate the dead mouse. Its soft amber fur, its plump white belly. Pregnant maybe? I am supposed to be tidying the garden, cutting the grass, doing the jobs we soon won't have time to do. I'm trying to pull my weight, to take on all the practical things I can to prepare our house and our lives before what happens next. I hate the dead mouse because it reminds me of everything I fear I cannot do. If I cannot move this dead mouse, I reason, I cannot deal with other gruesome things, a tyre-flattened badger on the side of the road, giant furry moths trapped in the lampshade at bedtime. I want our children to see the world bounce off me, to be strong and practical and unflappable.

A dad, I think, would pick up the dead mouse.

⊛

The next antenatal class brings a new development: we're going on a school trip. Giddy at being released from the confines of the community hall we are told to rendezvous at a house near the rowing lake. We cram into the front room, five of us on each of the two small sofas. No mean feat when half of the people are heavily pregnant. The class this week is led by Zara, a local midwife and breastfeeding expert, whose own school-aged children find every imaginable excuse to sneak into the room, overwhelmed with curiosity about the strangers in their house and the opportunity to see bare breasts. Zara celebrates mothers'

bodies, what they can produce, what they can endure. For the
first time I feel self-conscious in mine, suddenly too bony, too
empty, in a room full of rounded bellies and milky breasts. We
start with ice-breakers, party games, in which we're made to
drink water backwards from a cup to see how difficult it is for
babies to breastfeed in awkward positions. We all play along with
this nonsense, partly because we are worn down, low on dignity.
Partly because there is no time to waste in maintaining self-
respect. The babies are coming. Week by week the due dates are
getting closer. There is something else that's different about this
week's class. For the first time, a medical professional sees me not
as an awkward exception, but simply as a soon-to-be parent. Zara
asks me if I've considered induced lactation, offers to put me in
touch with a consultant.

—It's perfectly possible for you to breastfeed without giving
birth if you want to, she says, and writes me out a list
of herbal supplements.

It's not a baby, it seems, but the peaks and troughs in hormones
that create that particular miracle. The idea that I could
breastfeed the babies opens something up, another possible type
of motherhood. I don't want to, but still, her question clarifies
something, helps me to understand why the classes have been
so difficult. Paula has shown us a motherhood that begins and
ends in the body; everything else is logistics and administration.
Carry the bag, drive the car, call the grandparents. A clerk to
the family. So it is powerful, this news, that my body could do
the work of feeding a baby, just as it will do the other work of

motherhood. I know that mothers don't always qualify by giving birth, some mothers join a family later, some mothers adopt children, some children adopt mothers. Their bodies make sacrifices too. There are tolls on the arms that reach down and lift up, strains on the backs that sleep on the floor beside a cot, pains in the legs that chase and kneel. There's something else too, deep inside the body. A new gland that grows near the heart, releasing new instincts and a lifetime of worrying. Zara gives me permission to think again.

Reminds me that my body will also work for our babies.

Reminds me that mothers are more than bodies.

◦

In early summer I have to travel to Ireland for work. At the airport, I join the line for security and affect the appearance of a frequent business traveller, placing my belt and phone in the plastic tray with visible ennui, queuing up with all the sleepy men and women holding their shoes. Strangers bound together by the border guard's patting hands, the secrets of their dandruff or athlete's foot revealed to each other in clear plastic bags.

The traffic is heavy through Dublin and the airport bus crawls past the city's landmarks. I've seen it all before, the grey college, the white cast-iron bridge, but this evening everything is unfamiliar. The city is sharpened, dressed for battle over the marriage equality referendum. Banners the size of buildings.

small

People wearing their votes on T-shirts and badges. Yes. No. Yes.
The bus moves slowly beside the river and I sit at eye level with
the posters lashed to each lamppost. Every few metres, pictures
of soft-skinned toddlers and blue-eyed babies, actual poster
children.

                                                        No.
            She needs her mother for life, not just nine months.
                                                        No.
            Children deserve a mother and a father.
                                                        No.
                A mother's love is irreplaceable.
And this assumption that when a man wants to marry another
man it is solely in order that they might raise a family strikes me
as oddly prim. As if legitimacy of children is the only thing at
stake.
There are many more posters campaigning for No than Yes.
The money.
As the bus follows the river out of the city the message is clear.
                                            No. You are not equal.
                                            No.
            You are not fit to be a parent.
                                                        No.
You are not welcome here. I think about what it must be like to
pass these posters every day on the way to work, or school. These
posters have many messages.

                                            No.
Spend a few more years pretending you're in love with a footballer

instead of the girl in your history class.

No.

Live another decade watching how you dress.

No.

Make that a lifetime of being married to your career, people will
understand you just never found time to meet the right person.
Newspapers publish stories to counteract the posters. Dignified
old men in flat caps and women who look like your grandmother,
speaking up at last.

We have always been here.

Young people take the cue to come out too, defiantly holding
hands, desperate for people to notice, half-hoping they won't.

Because it still isn't done lightly.

People care enough to pay for these posters, care enough to string
them up from lampposts.

I sit back in my seat and turn away from the window as the bus
joins the motorway and drives on to Galway.

When the conference is over I travel back to Dublin to spend a
few days researching in the National Library. It is, I realize, one
of the last times I will truly be on my own. The reading room is
too quiet after the days of conference gossip and it takes me an
hour to tune out the sound of other readers coughing, fingertips
quietly tapping on keyboards. I spend my mornings in the cave
of a microfiche machine, scrolling and scrolling through tapes
of old periodicals. In the afternoons, I look at journals, printed
during the paper rationing of the Second World War, the paper

flecked with greens and blues from the previously pulped books they are made from. I eat my lunch alone in a cafe near the library and when the reading room closes I walk through the city and buy the last ticket for the opening night of a play.

◉

For the final antenatal class, Paula gives us dolls to play with. She teaches us how to wipe their plastic bottoms and change their fake nappies. When the dolls are all dressed, the 'dads' must practise holding them. Mothers have instincts, innate powers to nurture and hold. The rest of us will need to learn how to hold our greatest love without dropping it. So, I sit, with my two pretend babies nestled in the crook of each arm, listening to this woman and her parting advice on encouraging an overdue baby to come into the world.

—The best thing, she declares, is to get the baby out the way
     it got in.

I consider the logistical challenges of conducting microscopic procedures on the kitchen work surface and decide, on balance, we'll just have to wait.

mercies

It is a strange thing to watch the person you love, sitting under a
tree,

       pregnant,

           paused.

                  Familiar and new all at once.

All through the summer we have made this our Saturday spot,
armed with newspapers and takeaway coffee.

                           Biding our time.

Waiting it out in the shade of horse chestnut trees.
We sit in layers of ourselves, in and around each other, counting
the long weeks until we are due to meet. The strange in-between
days as one life starts to pass into memory. A new life on its way,
still unreal, still imagined. We watch the people walking on the
long straight path, a busy procession of couples holding hands,
parents pushing prams or chasing toddlers on scooters. Soon, we
say to each other. Soon.

A young couple breaks off from their tour group and comes to
settle on the edge of our tree's shadow. We exchange our stranger-
smiles, nod a welcome.

—Nice weather, the man observes, in a manner strangely
rehearsed. A phrase suggested perhaps in his guidebook, under
the heading: talking to the locals.

—You've been to the castle? I reply, gesturing at the bags from the
gift shop.

And we talk for a few minutes, about Texas, where we have never

small

been, but have a friend, would love to, one day. We talk about the
trains, for which we are sorry, and the views, for which we take
proxy credit. They loved the castle. Their favourite part was the
dolls' house. It is everyone's favourite part.

The idea is appealing, the Queen's huge castle, pregnant with
a tiny house fit for a Queen. Everything in it perfectly scaled,
one foot to one inch. Real running water, real electric light,
real fine wine in real miniature bottles. The library packed
with six hundred books the size of postage stamps. It's a feat of
craftsmanship but there's something unsettling too in the ratio
of work to output. The monograms on the bedlinen are said to
have taken almost two thousand hours to complete. How small
was the needle? How fine the thread? Beth lays back on the grass,
her head resting on my legs, and I think of the months that have
passed between now and all the unimaginable smallness of their
beginnings. How strange it seems already, the focus on the tiny
cells that have grown so quickly into great lumps of baby, their
elbows and feet bulging through Beth's dress. Clouds cover the
warmth of the sun and we decide to walk home. I help her up
from the grass. My arms full of her and our small daughters.

In the last weeks of summer, Beth arrives home from work each
day, hot and swollen in her new body. She spends the evenings in
the garden, wedged into a deckchair, her feet and ankles cooling
in the water of an inflatable paddling pool. Between breakfast
and bedtime the bump has grown again.

Soon, she won't be able to reach the steering wheel.
                              Her shoes don't fit.
She cannot sleep, even with the windows wide open and the
electric fan pushing cool air across the bed.
              She is sometimes miserable, sometimes euphoric.
                              She carries on.
She grows.

She misses things,
a friend's wedding,
a college reunion,

                                        her feet.

In August I take a few days off work, put the radio on, and set
to work decorating the babies' room. I assemble a wardrobe,
a changing table, two cots. I spend a weekend sanding every
surface and blunting every corner so the spare room meets the
safety standards of a secure psychiatric unit.
Not the spare room,

                              theirs.

A place for them.
Their home.

My pregnancy tracking app tells me that the babies can now
blink. They are able to recognize light and dark. They have
started dreaming. All of these new things that make them seem
more real, the alarming pace of change. The process is a stand-off

now, their growing bodies pushing Beth's to its limit. The email marking thirty weeks brings a new possibility, describing for the first time what would happen if a baby was born now. Possible but not advisable. The babies' lungs are not yet mature enough, they wouldn't be able to breathe on their own, the app says, their bodies are too small to regulate temperature. Our daughters are still first drafts, recognizably human but not yet ready to survive in the world.

Not yet, we tell them.
> **Not yet.**

At thirty-one weeks, the babies can recognize both our voices. We sing and read to them, but there's no need. They've already been listening.
They know us already.

⊛

In the evenings we walk in large figure-of-eight loops around the fields opposite our house, yellowing grass and light sky. It is the midway point of the school holidays and a group of teenagers have tied a rope underneath the bridge, swinging from it into the cold river water. Others climb above the sign which reads NO SWIMMING, NO DIVING, and jump from there. They swim to the soft steep banks, wading through knee-high grass, and go round again. As we walk, Beth and I talk more seriously about names, following the footpath around the fields testing initials and middle name combinations. We try to think of names just right for twin sisters. We talk about the parents we might be, firm but not too strict? Kind.

We both see it then, as we circle back round to the bridge. The scene at the end of the footpath all wrong. Too many people. Yellow police tape, high-visibility jackets. An ambulance on the towpath. Two boys and a girl, shivering and wet. A police officer stands at the entrance to the footbridge, directing dog walkers and joggers to take the long way round. The bridge is closed, our route home off limits. So Beth sits on the grass, settles her back against a tree, takes off her shoes. We can wait. Perhaps it isn't as serious as it seems. Turn away. Be patient. But the policeman spots us; the last thing he needs is a woman going into labour out here. So I point out our house to him, visible from the bridge, the one with the green door. He knows it's too far to send us round the other way, a loop of two miles to avoid the river, so he escorts us, over the bridge, above the bubbling of the police divers.

The next morning a journalist knocks on the door, asks did we see anything, did we know the drowned boy.
—Have you got any children? she asks me, do you let them play
     by the river?
And I don't know why I say,
—No, they're too young, which is technically true but
     also absurd.

small

But I cannot undo it. Unsay it.

—Sorry, no. I didn't know him.

I take her card and close the door.

I didn't tell her I had seen his friends, dripping and sobbing, forcing down the tea my neighbour had brought out to them. I didn't tell her about the stretcher.

The blanket.

I couldn't tell her about the car that pulled up behind the ambulance.

The backs of his parents' heads as they followed the policeman.

®

We are wrong about the long wait.

One Saturday in early September the babies announce their intention to arrive, too early. This is the weekend we had planned to pack the hospital bag, not the weekend we'd expected to use it.

Beth calls to say her waters have broken, as my train rushes in the opposite direction.

A call that deletes a day, changes all plans.

A call that leaves me waiting, how long can it have been? Minutes only, for the train to reach the next station so I can reverse my journey.

As the new train spools me back towards home I read, frantically, the last chapters of the baby book on my phone. Cramming for

my exam. I read all the pages I have been avoiding.
Holes in the heart.
Sepsis.
Still birth.

At the hospital the nurse explains that it is all a question of
timing now.
They bring Beth an injection, steroids to mature the four scale-
model lungs growing inside her.
Every extra hour the babies stay inside Beth's body improves the
maturity of their lungs, but also increases their risk of becoming
distressed now the amniotic sack has been punctured.

    Do we seem as afraid as we are?
    As lost? Nobody mentions it.

Propped up on the hospital bed, Beth's round belly is a cartoon
bomb, the fuse fizzing shorter and shorter by the hour. I try to
comfort or distract her, to talk over the sounds of other women
vomiting or crying out in pain. I read her the news headlines but
we don't care about the world anymore. I ease her wedding ring
off her finger with Vaseline because the midwife asks me to. Just
in case. I linger in the green glow of the cubicle until it is late and
the midwives insist I leave the three of them until morning. So I
find a way to walk out of the ward, along the corridor and into my
car, to our house, and our bed.

small

◉

On Sunday we wait.

                               Their hearts beat.

     Her eyes close.

I watch.

     We wait.

The midwife comes in. Checks. Goes out.

The midwife comes back. Checks. Goes out.

                               Their hearts beat.

     She is hungry.

     She is tired.

We are frightened and nervous and ready and not.

I adjust the surgical stockings preventing blood clots forming in her swollen legs, fetch her a piece of toast from the labour ward trolley.

Yesterday was a day of action and hurried journeys.

Today we are almost settled, resigned to living here in this hospital cubicle.

We adjust our expectations, make pulse rates our hobby, whispering our main employment.

                  Waiting is familiar now.

                  There's relative safety in it.

                               Until something changes.

A baby in distress.

A warning sign.

A change in atmosphere.

They move us across the corridor into to a private room, and into the care of Clara, a young Italian midwife. She has two pens in her breast pocket, the kind with multiple nibs which click down to write in black, blue, red, or green. This comforting detail. She has eight potential pens at her disposal; Clara is ready for anything. We learn that Beth is in the queue for an emergency Caesarean and so we wait as bigger emergencies push her down the list, or wait for her case to become more serious and outrank less major ones.

We are not the only ones living through this story today.

It begins now.

The real separation of it.

This part of it that is only hers and theirs.

Beth closes her eyes and goes somewhere I cannot follow, a place of focus and readiness.

Do the babies do the same? Do they sense that it is time, do they brace themselves for what comes next? All the things they overheard at the antenatal classes.

I watch her, her eyes closed, breathing, concentrating, and imagine weaving a golden thread around her, wrapping the three of them in a cocoon of my protection.

I hold her hand. I stroke her hair out of her eyes.

And I pray my desperate nonbeliever's prayers for all I'm worth.

small

At three o'clock Clara sends me to the canteen.
—You'd be surprised, she says, how much time we have to spend
        on partners passing out.
So I go and stand by the chilled cabinets, contemplating which
hospital sandwich is most suitable for marking the birth of one's
children.
I decide cheese and ham.
When I return to the delivery room Clara and two other nurses
are working busily around Beth's bed. In the few minutes I was
gone the waiting stage finished; it is our turn to go through to the
operating theatre.

After all the years of trying,
                    all the months of pregnancy,
        we are in the final hour of being just the two of us.

Beth is a warrior ready for battle. I am in fancy dress as a doctor,
trying to swallow a mouthful of dry sandwich before the world
turns upside down.

The pre-surgery visits begin.
        Surgeon,
        Anaesthetist,
        Paediatrician.

One at a time they enter the room, like supplicants approaching
the royal bedside. Bearing their news and checking their notes,

as if a woman bursting with babies is in a position to request a second opinion on what is ailing her. And as each medic reads their lines, we nod and say we understand as if some alternative is possible. The total transition of power reduced down to a few lines;

> consent forms,
> warnings,
> allergies.

Next of kin.

Finally, the paediatrician comes to talk to us, the man who will take care of our daughters as soon as they are born. At his side, a red-headed junior doctor, obviously thrilled to be involved in a complex case at last.

—*Babies who are this small, the paediatrician says, have a good chance of survival.*

Small is not good for babies.

It is not whimsical or cute or the cause of admiration.

It is the first time it occurs to us that they might not survive.

®

small

The surgeons place a curtain of blue material between us and
them. A surgical drape pinned up vertically from Beth's chest
so she cannot see her abdomen as it is sliced open. The operating
theatre is busy with people and purpose and all I can do to help
is hold her hand and pretend with everything I've got that it will
be alright. I am not prepared for a day like today – the antenatal
classes only taught me cheerleading; squeezing sweaty hands
and rubbing tired back muscles through the tearing strains of
labour. I sit quietly beside Beth's head, holding her left hand, and
I try not to look up, her unzipped body reflected above us in the
surgical lights. Distorted in the curve of glass and lights,
red enough.

All I have is quiet word after quiet word to drop into her ear.

> The day we walked on a glacier.
>
> The stones, that became ice, that became the surface
> of the moon.
>
> The photo we have from that day, do you remember it?
>
> Huddled together in an ice cave the shape of an eye.
>
> An excursion to another world. People we had been once.
>
> A place as far away from here and now as possible.

And the room is full of mumbling numbers.

Heart rate and blood pressure and minutes on the table.

A room of people working or waiting.

Until the anaesthetist says to us,

—Ready? It's now.

Our daughter does not cry, as she comes into the world.

The doctor passes her overhead to more waiting blue-gloved hands.

She is dark red and floppy and, it seems, dead.

—She's fine, she looks absolutely fine, I hear myself say to Beth as I watch, and try not to watch, the doctors helping her to breathe. So many hands, hands the size of her whole body, rub and check and prod her.

There is whispering and bustling as she is wrapped and warmed, and we are allowed just a glimpse as she passes by in her heated cot to intensive care.

I force my eyes to look, to see her frowning blue-purple face. She is wrapped so tightly in hospital blankets that we cannot see if she is moving, the oxygen mask over her face so small it must be a toy.

There is no time to pause. As our first daughter is wheeled out of the room, our second is lifted high above the operating table, cleaned and wrapped and checked. She is a touch stronger, the doctor says, and well enough to rest a moment on Beth's pillow. We meet her, this tiny girl with bright eyes, already wearing her doll-sized hat. The surgical nurse writes the times of their births on the whiteboard, four minutes and two seconds apart.

Twin I and Twin II.

—Take a picture on your phone, he urges me, those minutes will make all the difference in a few years.

◉

small

Then we are apart. The four of us separated in different parts of
the hospital. Blasted into fractions of the whole.
I wait, alone, in a hospital corridor, as the medics attend to Beth
in the operating theatre. The babies are sent to two separate
teams, doctors and nurses huddled around their cots.
—Wait here, a nurse tells me.
        —I'll come and find you when it's time.
So I wait, in the corridor of the Neonatal Intensive Care Unit,
reading the letters pinned to the wall. I read them all. Pocket
biographies of all the daughters and sons who lived out their
whole lives on this ward. Weeks or days or hours. There is no time
to waste in adjusting,
I learn the lesson quickly.

                              Babies die from smallness.

I walk softly when they call me into the ward, a roomful of
babies, sleeping through the flashing lights, the beeps and clicks
of the machines that are keeping them alive. In the far corner of
the room I find them, side-by-side in their incubators, and I learn
how to tell them apart by all the small things the hospital has
stuck on or into them. Twin II has a tube stuck to her face with
ovals of tape, the wires to her heart monitor are yellow, and the
bedding the nurses have placed her on are printed with teddies.
Twin I seems smaller, her legs curled up to her chest. She has
a splint on her arm, more hair, and her oxygen tubes are stuck
down with tape squares.
—Hello you two, I whisper into the space between them.

—You're still together, I say. Don't worry.

Because they seem so far apart from each other after all this time so closely bound together.

—Mama's ok, I say. She's just along the corridor. She'll be here to see you as soon as she can.

—And I'm here. It's ok. Mummy's here.

And for the first time,

I am.

I take what I can back to Beth who is wired and tubed in her own hospital bed on the surgical recovery ward. I show her pictures of the babies on the screen of my phone. Two blurry dolls in plastic boxes who are, it seems, our daughters.

I don't tell her about the letters pinned to the corridor walls.

She is to be transferred to the postnatal ward for the night, a long room of new mothers, wreathed in babies and buttered toast. Our babies will stay where they are, two floors down in intensive care, and I will run between them. They are so close, really, all in the same building, but it is all the distance in the world for a mother who has just given birth to babies she cannot hold or see. I take Beth's first messages of love to them and bring back more photos of tiny hands and feet in return.

Space babies, curled tight in their futuristic pods. Modern incubators are remarkable pieces of equipment, they have heat pads and cooling systems to control and regulate the baby's temperature. Movement censors, and humidity controls.

small

Yet even with all this scientific wizardry, at night, nurses place hand-made quilts on top of them, tucking the babies in like budgerigars.

It seems obvious now, that a baby born too soon feels the cold when not wrapped in layers of womb and mother. The early incubators, inspired by boxes used to warm exotic eggs in the Paris Zoo, were built of sturdy wood, packed with sawdust for insulation, and heated by hot water tanks. Babies lay in baskets, four per incubator, side-by-side like cannelloni. The mortality rate fell, babies who had been expected to fade away had kept warm, and, therefore, lived. Still, hospitals were doubtful. Was warming babies really medical? Why waste time on hopeless cases. On runts. Isn't smallness nature's way of saying who will and will not survive the trial of birth? Modern incubators developed, not in hospitals, but as a travelling exhibition, a Coney Island side show. Roll up, roll up, to see the unbelievably small babies.

At one in the morning a nurse tells me to go home.
—Tomorrow, she says. That's when they'll need you.
      —Go home. Sleep.

Our house has become a museum of a different life.
It is too late to call anyone, too lonely to open champagne.
I make a cup of tea and drink it in the bath.

people

Premature babies are the smallest people.
Precious artefacts kept in glass boxes.
Too thin.
Too fluffy.
Unfinished.

If their skin is strong enough, premature babies wear 'tiny baby' clothes, newly born but not quite newborn.

Their hair, if they have any yet, is stuck down, unwashed to their apple heads.

They wear size 0 nappies like junior supermodels.

Oxygen flows through tubes in their nostrils, vitamins and antibiotics through tubes in their mouths. Probes and monitors measure their heart rates, blood pressure, temperature.

They wear security tags on their ankles, like criminals.
Small bodies surveilled.
Surviving.

When the babies cry, the noise is muffled inside their incubators.
Hardly heard.
When the parents cry, they turn their heads to shoulders or sleeves. Hardly seen.

small

They keep the smallest people in a room that is like no other place you have been. The soft silence of a dozen sleeping babies, the noise of countless machines bleeping, pumping, checking. All the bustle and busyness of rubber shoes squeaking on the floor, hushed phone calls, trolley wheels, taps running. The machines that monitor the undercooked babies are musical, ding-dong doorbell chimes on electro beats, filling the room with space-age lullabies.

Until,

in a missed breath
or paused heartbeat,

the monitors flash red lights.
A change to the melody that brings nurses running.

Because breathing, it turns out, is something very small people have to learn.

Babies born before breathing comes naturally, the connection between brain and nervous system not quite in place. So the nurse reaches a gloved hand inside an incubator, remarks with ease that a baby 'just forgot to breathe for a moment', rubs them on the chest, rebukes them with,
—Come on little one, did you forget something?
A slip-up. A lapse in concentration.

The first person to call me mummy is a nurse wearing a black

headscarf and green scrubs. Back in the dark cave of beeps and
lights, she turns to me with a clipboard and says,
—Mummy, we'll need nappies, cotton wool and their clothes.
When I realize she means me I manage to nod.
—Do you have names yet? she asks. We need them for their
           charts, otherwise it'll stay as Twin I and Twin II.
We have known their names for a month or so, tested them out
on the back of envelopes, trialled them privately around the
house. I introduce the babies to the nurse, bringing them into
being all over again.
—Lovely, she says, as she carefully copies their names onto the
laminated signs above their incubators, labelling the exhibits in
her strange gallery.

◉

The NICU is divided into three rooms: sickest, sicker, sick. Over
the days or weeks or months babies spend here, they graduate
from room to room. Growing bigger. Moving towards home.
Most do. Some.
Home is a whispered word here, a mythical place that premature
babies dream about. The place their parents disappear to. For
overdue showers and hastily prepared meals. For a few hours'
sleep.
The first days pass and we learn
the rules of this strange new land.
Hands must be washed and coats removed.

small

Voices lowered.

             Hearts strained.

We learn where to park the car and what to avoid in the canteen.
We learn about the youthful arrogance of the junior doctors we
are dependent on and the unflappable resilience of the nurses
working long and tiring hours.
Days pass and we forget.
What life was like last week. Who we were before.
**How we had imagined this would be, the beginning of our life
as parents.**
Two days after the birth, Beth is discharged from the hospital.
She is no longer a patient so now we will both have to leave our
babies at the end of each day, tucking them in, kissing their
incubators goodnight. Call any time, the nurses tell us, so
we do, phoning the ward at two or three in the morning. For
reassurance. Because we are awake anyway. Everything is the
same, the night nurses tells us. No change.
And though we know we should sleep, it isn't easy, in this house
full of baby things, the cots, the car seats, the plastic bathtub. All
empty and unused.

The worst of it:

       the way she wakes in the night, sweating, panicking,
       reaching for babies who are not there.
The habits we have to break:

       talking to the bump that has gone.

The impossibility of these babies:
        here and not.

                        ®

You would not call it beautiful, the hospital. All its concrete
and glass. The cracks in the hallway floor taped down. The
windows painted shut. But there is comfort in the familiar. The
hospital-coloured walls, plaster pink, pastel green and grey. All
the wipe-clean chairs and vending machines. For the first time
I appreciate the lines painted on the floor, a reminder that the
hospital understands, you cannot raise your head when you are
ill, or weary, or frightened. Follow the green line growing under
your feet, the hospital will lead you to where you need to go.
For the first sixteen days of our babies' lives Beth and I don't go
anywhere but the hospital and our house. A tiny new geography
of bed, car park, ward, canteen. One Sunday morning we
discover there's a second coffee cart serving the emergency
entrance to the hospital so we go on a special outing. Striding
along the corridors together, conquistadors with lattes.

We learn that evenings are the busiest times on the neonatal
ward. As the night shift starts, dark-eyed new parents return to
the hospital, proffering their little fingers through the portholes
of incubators, passing on the news of the day. We learn that each
family takes their turn to be the newest. Mothers with cannulas
still taped to the backs of their hands. Limping. Sore. Fathers

85

in crumpled shirts. All the fear and unfairness of it written on their faces. We watch as they become experts too, explaining to the next new parents which alarms to worry about and which to endure. It happens faster than you would think, our submission to the institution. The way the hospital absorbs us all into its bloodstream.

We learn that, despite it all, we are lucky. It might have been worse, it often is. So many things can go wrong with such small people. The parents adjust, reshape themselves to fit around a baby who is unexpectedly early or incomprehensibly sick. And with it comes a new mistrust in the world. None of us have been spared. Sometimes we gather together in groups, in the corridor waiting for the ward security doors to open, or standing in line to pay for the car park. We try to talk to each other but none of us can remember names, or think of what to say. We are all tired, sick of hospital canteen food, wearing strange outfits thrown on in the few moments we have at home. Two mums and two babies. The teenagers ('just babies themselves', people whisper as they leave the room), who are told off by the nurses for racing wheelchairs in the corridor. A woman whose baby is stiff and trembling with withdrawal, who folds her son's clothes so carefully, but is gone by the time the social worker comes to pack them into a bag for him.

◉

Beth's sister comes to visit the babies, somehow finding her way to the hospital, which is miles from any train station. She arrives bearing a pink balloon, an enormous bunch of flowers, and two teddies, all of which are confiscated by the receptionist as possible infection risks. When she peers in at them she sees what we no longer can, how small they are, how sick they look, how scary the ward is. She touches her fingertips to the edge of the incubator and joins the list of people who will always love them.

◉

Smallness is the problem here but it is also the solution. Small adjustments in pressure, or heat, or antibiotics. Small additions that make huge differences.

Small margins of hope.

One morning I arrive to find a junior doctor preparing one of our babies for a blood transfusion. Her blood is too thick, the doctor says, it's moving too slowly around her tiny body. I watch as they squeeze her hand like a ball of dough, trying to raise a vein, stabbing at her just-made skin.

I might like to wait outside, the doctor suggests, it won't be nice to watch. But I tell her I'll stay, ask if I can help. The doctor puts me to work, hands me a pair of latex gloves and shows me how to feed the baby sugar water from my fingertip. Not a painkiller, just a distraction. As they work, her tiny tongue flicks at the droplets, a bee not a baby. The doctors, all giants, talking across her incubator.

◉

And I wonder if all the nurses know that I am falling in love with them?
If they can tell by the way I watch them work that I would take their tired heads in my lap and thread my fingers through their hair to thank them? That I would hold tight to the hands that handle our babies with such care. Kiss the tips of the doctors' ears as they work like watchmakers, squinting through an eyeglass to find an impossible vein, threading a wire from heel to heart.

◉

The babies are hospital patients but they are also just babies. While the medical staff manage the oxygen in their blood or scan their brains for abnormalities, Beth and I tentatively enter parenthood. We learn to change nappies through incubator portholes, dipping cotton wool into a bowl of sterile water, wiping tiny bottoms in nests of wires and blankets. Every millilitre of milk in, every wet or soiled nappy out, has to be recorded on the clipboards hanging at the ends of their incubators. We clean our fingernails like surgeons, we fold and refold spare blankets, we learn how to hold the tiny syringes of

milk, linking them to the feeding tubes in their noses. We try to
wear shirts we can unbutton so that we can hold our daughters
against our chests, warming them with our skin. The nothing
weights of them, one girl a bag and a half of rice, the other, two
bags of sugar.

And there is often confusion.

Cases of mistaken identity.

Not between the twin sisters, who are labelled securely at ankle
and wrist.

But their mothers, who break the rules by being plural.

This muddling.

The nurse who thinks I am their aunt.

The nurse who thinks Beth is a surrogate.

*

We settle into an evening routine, home to eat, then back to the
hospital for a few hours before bed. As the weeks go by we stay
later and later, in part because it becomes harder to leave our
babies. In part because of what happens to the ward at night.
Each night is a victory now, another day survived, another day
closer to home. But nights here are something else too, stiller,
softer, than the days. No ward rounds, no visitors, no procedures.
Only the quiet routines of night feeds to punctuate the hours.

Each evening, the night nurses arrive like cavalry, taking
handover notes, waving their daytime colleagues home to dinner,

a hot bath, their own lives and their own problems. At night our babies transfer into the care of a remarkable double-act: Sandy, an unflappable matronly woman, and Emily, a student nurse. In the quiet moments of those nights Sandy educates us. She shows us the most efficient way of putting a squirming baby inside a vest. She shows us how to bring up wind, not by resting a baby over a shoulder, a reckless practice, but my perching her on a knee, hand under chin like a ventriloquist. Every night, at ten o'clock, an alarm sounds on her phone, a chorus of ducks quacking, to remind her it is time to turn on all the taps on the ward. The process, she tells us, is essential to maintaining the Victorian plumbing system.

On the nights we can't bear to leave the babies, Beth and I sit beside them as they sleep and Sandy trains us up. Lessons in motherhood, not just for here, in this state of emergency, but afterwards. The very act of talking about it such a humane gift. Sandy restocks equipment cupboards and talks about her own family. Her son who didn't sleep through the night until he was seven. The drawing of a horse her granddaughter sent her through the post. As she files the night's paperwork she talks to us about school – do we think our daughters would like to be in the same class, what are the schools like near our house? The babies sleep through all of this, the planning and dreaming of their futures. I watch the lights of their monitors, the waves of their hearts beating. Steady. I am amazed by it, all the scientific progress, the medical expertise that has saved their small lives.

But I know, too, that Beth and I survive because Sandy speaks to us as if we all will.

We all work quietly on those nights. Beth feeds the babies in turn, resting their heads on the pillow across her lap. Sandy sets out a new cot in the far corner of the ward for a baby due to be transferred here in the morning. Emily moves a chair across the ward for the parents to share. A small locker for his things. I finish sewing the felt animals I am making for the mobiles that will hang above their cots when they come home. A pink rabbit. An orange fox. Emily looks at the babies, then at the two of us, —Who will they look like? she wonders aloud.

And we all agree they will look like themselves.
They will look like each other.

Emily tells us about her father, a man who moved to California when she was a baby. She sees him once a year, in August. On her break she shows us the roof of his house on Google Earth, rows of blue swimming pools seen from satellites.

®

I'm in the hospital canteen one morning when my phone buzzes with an alert, a new message from the pregnancy app. At thirty-five weeks pregnant, it says, the baby is starting to develop an immune system. This is a great time to take a few weeks off work with your partner, go to the cinema, go shopping. Spend time together before the baby arrives. I delete the app.

small

Nobody at the hospital wants to tell us how long the babies might have to stay, but we infer the worst when they put us on the list of people who no longer have to pay for the car park. Each day I walk to the main entrance to collect a special permit, officially stamped with the receptionist's pity. Each day I am tempted to ask her if this sympathy cuts the other way too. If they charge people extra for breaking a leg skiing, a premium for bringing it on yourself.

We try to take the nurses' advice, go out, don't rush, they tell us.
—You'll look back and regret not making better use of all this
        free time, they say, once the babies come home.

So, we risk an excursion, not to the cinema, but the council leisure centre, where we have made an appointment to register our daughters' births. A change of scene from the medical to the municipal.

It is easy to tell who is here for what, although everyone in the waiting room tries to conceal the boom and bust of their hearts. The kindness that is looking at our own shoes or out of the window. I read the noticeboard, a strange collage of humanity, phone numbers for grief counsellors next to timetables for mother and toddler groups.

Everyone waits patiently, what rush could there be? The real thing is done elsewhere, in rooms with flowers and cards. The birth and death. Still, this is the place where it counts. Like everyone else, Beth and I wait silently. We do not complain as the time of our appointment comes and goes. Even though every minute spent here is a minute not spent with our small babies.

Even though we know that every mile we travel further away
from the hospital is a mile further to travel back if they call us in
an emergency.

And as we wait, we watch the others, walking in, then out, of the
office. Holding hands. Holding babies. An elderly man and his
grown-up daughter who finish their appointment then stand in
the waiting room, with no idea of what they are supposed to do
next. Two people, so obviously bewildered to find themselves in
a leisure centre, on a Tuesday morning, telling a stranger that his
wife, her mother, is dead.

Our turn comes and the registrar calls us in. Her chair is too
low and she peers at us from behind the bulky computer on her
desk.

—You're here to register a birth, she declares brightly. Pleased, no
doubt, with the change of tone from her previous appointment.

—Actually, two births, I reply proudly, we've had twins.

—Well I don't have time to register twins, the woman snaps.

You'll need to book a double appointment and come back
another time.

And as she stands to show us out, Beth begins to cry. All that
she has stored up over the last few weeks, all the shock and
exhaustion and pain of it, are about to flood over this officious
woman and her extensive glass paperweight collection.

And, of course, she does not mind the crying, the registrar. Rare
is the hour that passes here without someone breaking down in
tears. Everybody who walks into her office has a good reason to
cry, an obligation even.

So I bargain. Appeal for clemency.

I try to explain to this woman that we have left two sick babies in intensive care for this. Ask if she might consider registering one baby for now, see how the time goes?

And as Beth fumbles for tissues in her coat pocket, gulps, breathes; the registrar sighs. She clicks the mouse, adjusts her chair, and turns towards us, a most gracious benefactor.

—Mother's name? she begins.

Five years ago, two hundred miles away from here, Beth and I had visited a different council register office, to make the final arrangements for our Civil Partnership. If we wanted any of the joy and solemnity of a wedding, it turned out, we would have to build it for ourselves. The council would provide the paperwork and a paragraph of legally binding prose, in exchange for the specified fee. The rest was up to us. In one way, having the freedom to write our own vows, to choose the poems and music that meant most to us, was liberating. In another, it was a burden, forcing us to find meaning in symbols and traditions that were not really our own. Beth was disappointed, she had wanted the Welsh song 'Calon Lân', a lyrical plea to be granted a pure heart, to play as we walked down the aisle. She had grown up with the song, considered it a part of her personal history, her culture. But the registrar decreed it a hymn so it could not be so much as hummed within the vicinity of our secular wedding.

Now, years later, as we sit opposite this registrar, feeding her the details she needs about our daughters' births, I am reminded of that meeting. The familiar feeling of facing an official who has forgotten the people before them are real. To her, these certificates are simply more paperwork. But for us, they are protection, security, legal proof that we are a real family. She transcribes all the necessary information, our address, the name of the hospital, and unsurprisingly, since there are only nine letters and four minutes two seconds difference between one birth certificate and the next, proves quite capable of generating both forms in the allotted appointment time. As she prints out the official birth certificates, there is a surprising ceremonial flourish. From her desk drawer the registrar produces a fountain pen, heavy and gold-nibbed. She hands me the pen and I sign our daughters into reality, fixing them in language. Two new people. Made real at last.

In the car we sit for a moment, reading their names aloud. It is joyful to hold this evidence of our daughters in our hands. Official recognition of their first achievement; congratulations on winning joint first prize in the being-born competition. On our children's birth certificates Beth is designated 'Mother' and I am named as their 'Parent'. It is an odd solution to a legislative problem. Is the idea of two mothers or two fathers really so incomprehensible? The form has neutralized me. The functionality of it, the distance from reality, is unsettling. What does a parent do that a mother or father doesn't? Some combination of the two? A third way? No child ever called out in the dark for their Parent to rescue them from a nightmare. But Still, I'm more than a little grateful to be on the form at all.

◉

At the weekend my parents come to the hospital to meet the babies for the first time. I take photos on my phone to record the occasion, and when I look back at them I see that the camera angle makes them seem tiny, shrunken people. My parents, oddly small in the high-backed hospital chairs, hunching over their tiny granddaughters. Or, perhaps they were just smaller that day, diminished by the shift in the world order. We are the parents now.

The babies are still too small for any of the clothes we have bought them, so we dress them in the tiny cardigans and bonnets knitted by the kind old ladies who donate them to the hospital. The knitted clothes make the babies seem old-fashioned, lemon-yellow cardigans with puffed sleeves and scalloped-edge buttons. Sleeping in their hospital cots, dressed in Sunday best.
That Sunday afternoon I sit with one of the babies, feeding her lunch, connecting a syringe to the feeding tube in her nose and holding the few millilitres of milk above her head so that it will drip slowly down into her stomach. We are as alone as we can be, content together amid the activity of the busy ward. I watch her tiny fingers, the stretches and jerks of her arms, the way she settles into half sleep as she feeds. She is slow to adapt to life after birth, she keeps her legs bent up to her chest, not realizing yet that she

has a whole world to expand into. The short nurse with the red glasses walks across the ward towards us.

—So, she asks, leaning across my daughter, do you know who the
daddy is?

◉

The syringe becomes a bottle.

They start wearing normal baby clothes.

They move from incubators to warm cots, and from those to cots that are really just Perspex trays on wheels.

They are allowed a toy, one small brown rabbit each.

They start to look like babies.

They take naps side-by-side, the band back together at last. They are weighed and weighed, inching ever closer to some magic number the doctors agree is still small but big enough to be allowed home. Under careful supervision we give the babies their first baths, washing carefully around the black stumps of their umbilical cords. Taking photos of the glorious occasion, their indignant faces and round tummies, their long froggy legs in the warm shallow water. It is family life but not really. There is no privacy in a hospital, no rest, as we commute back and forth to parenthood each day.

Finally, we are invited to move into the hospital for a few days so we can help prepare the babies for coming home. We are thrilled to make it to the 'rooming in' stage, our first family sleepover and

a chance for all four of us to prove we are ready to take the final
step out of limbo and back towards normality. Sandy calls us
while we're at home packing.

—Bring your own sheets, she warns. All the hospital ones
      are rubber-lined.

Although Beth is on maternity leave, I have gone back to work.
Each morning I queue to use the ward shower, say goodbye
to the nurses as the shift changes back from night to day, and
drive to the university. Beth and the babies are bound up in the
hospital routine, ward rounds, feeding, monitoring. I spend the
day imitating myself. Students email me and I reply. Colleagues
ask me questions and I answer. I buy a coffee, or return a library
book, or teach a class, as if the whole world hasn't been entirely
transformed. In the late afternoon I drive back to the hospital, a
messenger from the outside world. When I walk onto the ward
the Scottish nurse tells me the babies have smelled of my perfume
all day since I kissed them goodbye that morning.

town

Three weeks before their due date, the hospital gives us
permission to bring our daughters home.

The final hours stretch out as we wait for the discharge
paperwork so I take one final walk to the coffee cart. I find myself
queuing behind the hospital chaplain and ask if I can pay for her
cappuccino, as if it might serve as some kind of down payment on
the debt I owe.

Our leaving, when it finally comes, is like the end of a holiday
romance. Send pictures. Don't forget to write. We'll always
remember you. Nurses cursing at the car seats as they fumble
with the buckles and straps. Cards and keepsakes packed away.
The tiny wrist bands that labelled them before they were named:

Twin I, Twin II.

The hats that will come to seem comically small.

Beth is still recovering from the Caesarean, lowering herself into
the car with a hand across her stitches. She cannot lift the weight
of the car seats yet so I carry one on each arm, the babies wrapped
up like Arctic explorers. Hats, mittens, snowsuits, although it is
only mid-October, the weather mild. As I drive the three of them
home I repel reckless drivers with a force-field of my will. It is the
longest short drive of our lives.

It is our first time alone with our children.

⁕

Of course it has been hard, all these weeks in hospital, all the
separation and worry. But for all that, the responsibility for

them was hardly ours at all. While the babies remained under the care of the hospital there was a delay in our authority. A delay in learning to trust our judgement, a delay in the physical contact between us all. As I drive I think of all those nights when somebody else lifted up our babies in the dark. Fed them. Held them when they cried. There is loss in that knowledge, regret at time missed. But there are incredible gains too, a new sense of trust in the world that we get from it all. A feeling that the world is peopled with heroes, people with the ability and willingness to help. People who did not love our babies but behaved as if they might, for all the hours they were in their care.

For the twenty minutes or so we are in the car the four us are nowhere, just in between. Between the hospital and home.

Between that life **and this.**

With all my new-parent enthusiasm I've prepped the car for this. Fitted sun shades on the back windows, a complex system of mirrors that allows me to see the babies in their rear-facing seats. My view is transformed on that drive, one rearview mirror showing me the road behind, the other our tiny scrunched balls of babies.

It is not nothing this small drive.

This unremarkable journey on unremarkable roads.

As I drive I glance into the mirror, this life-changing view, our babies, still smaller than newborns. A view to remember always and a vision of what that view will become.

All of us wondering if we are there yet.

world

And then it begins.

The four of us.
Real life.

And the pink cards on the mantlepiece. The 'It's a girl' balloons that have been slowly deflating in the hallway for the best part of a month.

We get on with it. Living in a way that had seemed so unimaginable for so long. The four of us in our own space, our own things around us. The luxury of sitting on the sofa in our pyjamas, eating bowls of pasta, the babies snoozing side-by-side in their carrycots. The greatest ever girls' night in.

On the third day at home a health visitor comes to the house. She gives us leaflets about cot death and weighs the skinny naked girls on the kitchen table. She asks about their feeds and the contents of their nappies. Pressing for detailed descriptions of the colour and texture of their shit in this brave new world where new rules of polite conversation apply.

—The yellow of that cushion or the yellow of that book cover?

she asks. And I make a mental note to throw both away. The health visitor drinks her tea, she doesn't mind it cold, and takes out her reading glasses to fill in her paperwork. The case has a red-and-white sticker on the lid: *'Some People are Gay: Get Over it'*. She asks us who will be the 'primary parent' so she can write it on the form.

Everything in the house is dangerous, she warns us. The whole place booby-trapped with sharp corners, hot surfaces, electrical

small

appliances. Bath water that might scald or drown. Plastic bags. Germs.

We're both at home for the visit because I've taken two weeks off from work. Paternity Leave, the form insists.
Two weeks for the four of us to be together. Learning. Worrying. Working it out. Two weeks for us to get to know how these babies work, without wires, or charts. The babies will teach you what to do, the health visitor tells us.

    Just listen.
        Just look.

                                          So we do.
Between the washing and sterilizing and feeding and winding and changing and bathing.
Sometimes, often, we set the babies down on the rug, side-by-side, and examine them as if they are a perplexing art installation.
Look, we say to each other, at the creases of their wrists,
      the absurdity of their tiny fingers.
Look at the way they turn towards each other,
      reaching out to touch.
Look at the way they sleep with their arms above their heads,
      in surrender.
Look at the way they stretch
      and yawn
      and frown.

                                  Look at them.
Listen to their small sounds, their growls and squeaks.

Look at them looking at us.

Wonder what they see.

A comforting blur. A source of warmth, food, transport.

We look at each other too.

New ways of seeing.

We watch each other doing new work.

For them. For each other.

The force of seeing each other surviving all of this.

New lusts in sick-stained sweatpants.

The smell of curdled milk.

A super-glue bonding,

melting skin onto skin. Fusing.

We make a web that criss-crosses between the four of us, binding
each to each, the parts to the whole.

All the gore of newborn nappies. All the night-time crying that
unleashes something new.

A reflex. A pain.

All the strange beauties of it beginning.

◉

Then a test.

After the first week at home it's clear that one of the babies won't
feed properly, she cries too much, she isn't gaining weight.

We call Zara, the breastfeeding expert from our antenatal classes,
and she makes a home visit. Standing in the kitchen she hooks

her finger inside the baby's mouth and diagnoses tongue-tie:
the flap of skin that links her tongue to her mouth is too short.
She can fix it, she says, if we come this Tuesday to her feeding
support group. The group meets in a hall where elderly people go
to practise their ballroom dancing in an inconvenient upstairs
room. We squeeze past the car park of prams and car seats to
carry the babies up the steep wooden staircase. The women who
run the group have taken breastfeeding to a semi-professional
level; when we arrive we have to step over the group leader who
is laid out on the floor, her three-year-old's jaws clamped around
her right breast as he runs a toy car up and down her stomach.
When he's finished he levers her breast back into her bra and taps
it proprietorially.

New mothers are clustered on the far side of the room in various
states of exhaustion and anxiety. Zara weaves between them,
adjusting the angle of a baby's head or the positioning of a
mother's elbows. The floor woman demonstrates again, this
time with her suckling toddler upside down, draped over her
left shoulder. It's hard to say whether anyone is encouraged by
the example. Beth holds one baby to her breast as Zara contorts
them into an advanced yoga pose while I carry the small patient
through to her appointment.
I bring the baby into the side room and set her down on the
changing table.
Zara holds her down,

                                    the other nurse snips.

—Take her back to feed now, they say. She'll be fine in a day or so.
Her bewildered crying. A betrayal of trust.
I pick her up and whisper an apology in her tiny ear.
The nurse wipes the blood from the scissors and hands them to me.
—These are your scissors now, she says. You can do whatever you
        want to with them.
As if, perhaps, I will find them useful for craft projects, or in case
I'm inspired to set up my own franchise snipping babies' tongues.
I take the scissors and pay her.

◦

At night, our daughters sleep in baskets, one either side of our
bed. Paper dolls, all in a row. When they wake to feed we have
midnight feasts, two bottles, two cups of tea.
However hard these nights are, they are so much better than
the nights spent without them. The nights we had to leave them
behind at the hospital. Each minute holding them is a chance to
catch up, writing over the lost time.
The sounds of them sleeping, the comfort of breathing each
other's air.
But there is fear too, sleeping beside their tiny clockwork hearts.
It is bad enough to imagine it, the miracle of their breathing
stopping in the night. Far worse when you've seen it happen before.

The mornings come in a fog of coffee and all the things that must
be done.

small

And then, the two weeks of my leave are over. It is time to go back
to normal life, or rather, to start an entirely new one. We prepare
ourselves to settle into some other way of being, and for now at
least, the health visitor was right, one of us will have to be the
primary parent because we will have to live out these months in
different ways and in different places.

Her days,

divided into small parts.

Hours that are bridges,

linking feed   to feed.

Nap   to nap.

The three of them, living in the blur of the present. Pasts and
futures far-fetched things.

All the new places where they spend their days, church halls and
community centres.

Seeking out others living this same strange life.

Comparing notes and filling hours until it's time to come home.

And when the three of them come back to the house, she sends
me photos. Small postcards from home and all their adventures.

Photos of the babies sleeping.

Photos of the babies in their pram.

A photo of one baby winking at the camera. A photo of the other
raising a fist in solidarity.

And for hours at a time I leave them, go back to my old life, and
live in it.

Driving to work along the same roads. Sitting at a desk or

standing in a lecture theatre. Reading. Speaking.

People ask after the babies, ask to see pictures on my phone.

So they can say,

—My next-door neighbour has twins.

Or,

—You've got your hands full now.

Or,

—Double trouble.

Or,

—Was it buy one get one free?

So I can smile, and shrug my shoulders in mock exasperation, and say,

—The more the merrier.

And, mostly, I am still myself.

And it's only once, or twice, that I have to lock my office door, make a pillow from my coat, and sleep on the floor, just long enough to remember how to drive home.

And as I leave each afternoon, I know that she is watching me, tracking the small blue dot that is me on the map.

Reinforcements. And I pause, just for a moment, in the car outside, taking a breath between one life and another.

Strange evenings we spend together, speaking our different languages.

The first months.

I come home from work and talk about meetings, deadlines,

colleagues, as if they are still things that matter. The politics of who said what in a committee. A reminder of all that she has put on hold. She talks to me about things I do not fully understand. How many millilitres of milk each baby had at her lunchtime feed. Their growth rates on the health visitor's chart. She is annoyed with me for not knowing the things she knows, for not keeping pace with expert opinion on tummy time, or the best brand of blackout curtains and if we should buy them.
So we argue about something. About nothing.

The temptation to resent each other's freedoms.

The greener grass.

One late afternoon in November I bump into a colleague, a famous novelist, as I'm leaving for home.
He has heard about the babies, offers his congratulations. He tells me I look younger, but tired.
—Most marriages can't survive children, he tells me.
    —You must cleave together, he says.
Whatever happens, cleave together.

◉

The next morning, our bedroom in half-light, I am woken, not by crying, but a quiet fidgeting of tiny legs. Small feet rubbing together. I prop myself up on my elbows to look into the Moses basket beside me and see my daughter, eyes wide open. Smiling. She hasn't called out, she remembers. She knows I am there.

Quietly, trying not to stir the others, I lift her out of her basket to rest her on the slope of my legs. We look at each other, we smile at each other, and I feel, for the first time, the weight of her complete faith in me.

You are meant to fall in love with a new baby; if you're lucky, it comes easily. The surprising part is when you first see that the baby loves you too. I think a lot during these first weeks about the baby books that tell me, a baby does not know, at first, that it is separate from its mother. I wonder what they make of us, of each other. Not four different people at all but some mutant sixteen-limbed being. Because we are all distorted in each other's eyes, that much is clear, all too close together to find perspective. All we can see. All that we are to each other. This is how it begins, the lopsided love between children and parents. A love that always flounders, in the end, on misplaced good intentions, on plans that should be called dreams. The baby and I look at each other.

We smile.

I understand that she will edge away from me, year by year.

That is how it works.

But, for today at least, we are all the other needs.

mouthfuls

The thing babies don't understand about routines is, it's really not about them.

In an attempt to preserve our sanity, we create systems to help us through the logistics of caring for baby twins. One adult, caring for two babies, is an equation that simply doesn't add up, there aren't enough hands. To create a false sense of control over this, we set up changing stations, upstairs and down, so one baby isn't left alone while the other is being hosed clean. Naps and feeding times are synchronized so both babies are kept to the same schedule. We keep spare dummies in the car for emergencies. We find solutions to the technical minefield that is bathing two babies at once. In all these early months Beth's expertise imposes order on the chaos. I am just an assistant, working my part-time shifts in the evening and weekends, slogging my way up to a promotion. It comes when the babies are six months old. Beth is going back to work and I am going to stop.
Six months of parental leave.
Six months of being in charge of *the routine*.

I can't wait to spend all of this new time with them, but as the date gets closer I worry that I might disrupt it all, prove myself to be the flaw in the system. Long days with babies is motherhood as we had imagined it. Both of us doing this work is a symbol of equality in our family, a mission statement for how we want our parenting to be. If we share the time off work, we think, we'll share the highs, and lows, of new parenting. Both witness first moments.

small

Smiles.

Steps.

Words.

We'll both get to feel how precious this time is.

How lonely.

We both know this much – going to work is not all drudgery and separation.
Work is also getting dressed, and feeling purposeful.
It is hot coffee, and real conversation, and clocked time.

Being an understudy is delicate work.
I prove myself ready, but not too eager.
She shows herself prepared for the change, but reluctant.
The magnetism of work and freedom.
The gravitational pull of the babies.
And mothers say to her,
—I don't know how you can do it, give up your time with
them like that.

A sacrifice.

A compromise.

And fathers say to me,
—I wish we'd done the same. Shared it. Made space for
each other.
We see it up close, the civil war between mothers, the pressure to stay at home, the expectation to go back to work. The measuring up and judgement. Each decision an apparent condemnation of the

other. And we spoil it for people with our muddling of the rules.
An embarrassment of mothers.
No model to lean back on,
no rank to pull.

It isn't a relay, there's no swift transition from Mama to Mummy.
We change lives by easing away.

By inching towards.

On my first full day at home I walk the girls into town. We
borrow books from the library. We buy milk. We come home the
long way, taking the path that follows the river, the pram wheels
clogging with mud. As we walk home I tell the babies the names
of the plants that grow near the water, marsh marigold, great
willow herb. They look out of their double pram at me, round
cheeks and wide eyes. Wondering, no doubt, what Mama would
say about this reckless disregard of the schedule.

I learn things quickly, how to feed two babies at once, how to
carry two babies upstairs at nap time. By Friday of the first week
it becomes clear that I have been misusing certain words all
my life; busy, say, or tired. I adjust to the change in perception,
the way that people talk to me as if I am an imbecile when I am
out with the babies. Speaking slowly and softly, as though the
simplest of questions might be too much. Learning to accept the
fact that the grown men and women who serve me in shops will
insist on calling me *mummy*.

small

◉

Instructions for leaving the house.

 Feed one baby.

 Wind the baby.

  Now, feed the second baby, wind her too.

 Change their nappies and place them in their bouncy chairs.

 Observe the babies daintily vomiting on themselves because you have put them in bouncy chairs so soon after feeding.

  Wipe their clothes and necks as if that will be sufficient.

   Sniff the babies.

     Admit defeat.

Change their clothes.

Next, pack the changing bag. You will need: nappies, wipes, cream, bottles, milk, bibs, cloths, jingly things, rattly things, cuddly things. Now, wrestle the car seats into the hallway and observe the weather. Curse the weather. Find snowsuits, gloves and hats. Dress babies in snowsuits, gloves and hats. Place babies in car seats. Realize one of the babies needs to have her nappy changed again. Consider joining in with the crying. Remove snowsuit, gloves and hat. Change nappy with no apparent resentment. Find your coat and purse. They are not where you left them. Realize you are still in your pyjamas. Rectify. Observe that the sun is now shining. Take babies out of car seats, swap snowsuits for cardigans. Next, spend a few minutes securing the car seats into your car. *Do* remember not to swear in front of babies. Do *not* start thinking about uninsured drivers. Get into the car. Get out again to retrieve the lost jingly thing that has been thrown on the floor. Remind the baby that if she wants the jingly thing so much she will need to hold onto it. Using your new rearview mirror, watch the baby immediately throw the jingly thing onto the floor. Start the engine. Realize that the baby sensory class will be finished before you get there. Consider other places you might go to on a Thursday morning with two small babies. Despair at the thought of all of them. Take babies back into the house.

Make coffee.

◉

I try my best to keep up with the routine.
I stick at the baby music class, the buggy fitness sessions, the various playgroups. I drop the baby yoga. I find my way to the places they have made their own over the last six months. I try to blend in, to step in where Beth has left off. The problem is, it feels, well, silly, to sit in a circle with other adult women, singing nursery rhymes for an hour. I cannot seem to settle into it. The women in the groups are raw, out in the world with their skin peeled off, sensitive to all the expectations of how they are supposed to do this. All the comments from strangers,

the wildly contradicting advice, the pressure to transform. In conversations by the tea urn they set down all the things they are carrying. The said and unsaid, measuring themselves against some fantasy version of motherhood, finding the reality harder, duller, stranger. Finding all this new love too much to bear. As the weeks pass I see that the groups are a place of camaraderie, a chance to witness and empathise. There's a safety in this shared experience, our moments of togetherness. Each week I take the babies to a twins and triplets playgroup. We all know what it has taken to get there, all the hours of washing and wiping. Twice. Three times over. Still the mothers are often on edge, ready to defend and protect.

Sitting beside a woman on a patchwork mat I try to compliment her baby.

—He's looking really well, I say, smiling.

—I'm not over-feeding him if that's what you mean,
     she roars back.

⊛

Home is a new place too.

     Re-made for fresh purposes.

Rubber ducks colonize the bathroom.

The space by the kitchen door is taken over by highchairs. The function of the house, shifted towards their needs and things. It isn't just the place, but the time that is new. The illicit thrill of being at home on a Monday morning when the rest of the world

slogs through a day of work or school. The three of us outside the
law, building towers with wooden blocks, knocking them down
again, while other people fill in their spreadsheets.
And on those days I am aware of how unusual it is,
to be this lucky.

To feel it.

Looking around at the life I had longed for, begged for.
Watching myself living it.

And on other days I am lost.
The loneliness of a kitchen at half past three in the afternoon.

The contradiction of it all.
Great bursts of happiness.
Hours of uncertainty.

⊛

The weather changes and I start to take the babies for long walks.
Walks that are really sleeps. The soothing motion of pram wheels
on pavement, the fresh air. I am just the engine, walking on
autopilot through housing estates, making circuits of suburban
streets, searching out routes with low kerbs and quiet traffic.
And each time I leave the house I think of it, the advice they
gave to children when I was at school. If you are lost, if you are
frightened, if a stranger is trying to give you sweets or show you a
puppy, always, always, look for a lady with a pram. A lady with a

small

pram, the teachers told us, is always a good person. Run towards
her, she will help you.
I wear my duties heavily when I am the lady with a pram.
Scanning the horizon for lost children, ready to swoop in
and rescue them from perverts or kidnappers. Ever vigilant.
Sometimes, as I walk, I pass other ladies with prams, and we look
into each other's tired eyes, knowing.

We are all seeing.

But unseen.

The great secret.

I had ignored them too, the invisible women. Pushing prams,

killing time.

Getting out of the house.
I know better now.
This new freedom to walk and observe.
When the purpose is the walk itself, no destination, no deadline.
A moving forward but not a going towards.

Just walking.

And I know that I can walk wherever I want now.
The power to trespass.
Transgress.
Because a baby is an excuse, a ready-made apology.
A lady with a pram is absolved of all suspicion. An invisible force
for good.

❀

And the worst thing is, I look at the clock.

When it is just the three of us, watering the tomato plants, or chalking our names on the path.
Even though I know these days are numbered. Even though I know that soon, this too will end.

Each day the babies become more fully themselves. More real. The future flashing across their faces like fast-changing weather. A raised eyebrow, a frown of concern, to make me think, yes, there you are.
I will see that face again and again.
Seven months, eight months, nine months, ten.
They edge out of their babyhoods, become new versions of themselves until it seems ridiculous that they were ever those scraps of skin and bone in incubators. These human puppies, chewing everything they can reach, playing for hours in cardboard boxes. The supermarket becomes their favourite excursion, the sheer sensory overload of the place, the chance to sit in the trolley seats, waving at strangers and clapping hands each time I take something from a shelf.
Today, a woman approaches us. It happens all the time, people in shops with time to talk. On the hardest days I seek them out, lingering in cafes, until the babies draw strangers over to us for a few minutes of comforting chat.
The woman reaches past me as if I'm not there and touches both babies on the back of their hands. Their fat little fists gripping the trolley handle.
—Oh how lovely, she says. Are they yours?

small

But there's no time to answer, she has something to tell us.
—I used to look after twins once. A friend of mine. She came
back from her holiday and she was enormous so I said,
either you're pregnant with twins or you've got your dates
wrong, and if it's twins I'll take the job! I looked after
them every day from seven in the morning until half seven
at night.

I am listening and smiling and making the sounds of a person
listening and smiling but I am not needed here. It is the telling
that matters.

—They moved away when they were six, the woman says, and
the thing is, you really do get so attached. One reminded
me of my own daughter and one morning, when I was
feeding them, I was just thinking, perhaps I loved one
more than the other, when the baby opened her eyes and
looked straight at me as if to say she understood, and I just
started to cry.

And, so, she does again, right there in the supermarket, next to
the rail of discounted bras.

Two sets of bewildered eyes peer up at me from the trolley.
                    If there's a protocol for this none of us know it.

change

There are days when you can see them growing.

      Coat sleeves creeping from wrist to elbow.

            Tables suddenly at head height,

                      new bruises on their temples to prove it.

Pregnancy is counted in weeks, infancy in months, childhood in years.

People talk in clichés because they are true.

The long hours and short years of parenthood. The first year of their lives condensed to the pace of a time-lapse camera. The blur of a flick book. All at once they are sitting, then standing, then taking steps. Balloons. Tricycles. Toddlers. And of all the things that surprise me, it is the talking that truly amazes. At two, each word they learn is a revelation, making language strange and pure. The ingenuity of sentences pared down to their bare bones.

      Shoes, help.

                      Up Me!

    No touch teddy.

Speech transforms them, but they have to work hard at it. Grasping at the handful of words they have, straining to be understood. I don't blame them for their tantrums when we don't bring the right cup, when we hand them the wrong toy. Imagine the agony of it, all the comprehension without the expression. The frustration of being outside language. I think of a weekend in Venice, years ago, just the two of us. The evening we took the water bus from The Lido back to San Marco, the air

so thick it broke into a thunderstorm. Rain battering the roof
of the boat. Lightning hitting the water like a movie. How I had
blundered attempts to make conversation with the people sitting
beside us. Piecing together the closest things I had to ask for the
word.
—What is your name weather light?
Back at the hotel I looked it up on my phone. *Un colpo di fulmine*,
a lightning bolt, the Italian for love at first sight.

Life stops being about nappies and bottles. Hair clips and
farm animals become the new currency. Our jobs change from
decoding cries to negotiating the requests that are now all too
clear. Bananas must be cut just so. Cheese sandwiches are to be
served on a yellow plate, even if, just yesterday, they would only
be eaten from a red one. Day by day they assert themselves in new
ways.
For well over a month one of the girls determines to wear a
swimming costume over her normal clothes. The other takes up
a signature mantra, shouting 'Oddybody, listen to me!' when
she wants everybody's attention, which is most of the time. The
playgroups that once felt strange feel like home. Under-heated
rooms of solidarity and company. I feel such gratitude for it all,
the little snack bowls and finger painting. The moment's rest and
gossip while the woman from the library sings nursery rhymes
with the children.

The days of carrying babies and pushing prams pass. Now,

we hold hands. Tightly on the stairs and loosely on the sofa. I am dragged by the hand towards a game, or a book that needs reading for the seventh time that morning. I am pulled away at the threshold of a new place. My hand is held carefully on pebbled beaches, firmly on the steps of a steep slide, faithfully at the side of the road. Their bravery is exhausting to watch. All the bumping into and falling over things. The tension between their confidence and my caution. Don't fall, climb down, not so fast.

When autumn comes round again the four of us walk together along the edge of the lake. Leaf crunching. Talking. We're hunting for conkers, twin ones, to take home where they will shrivel in a bowl. We look for acorns, admiring the pleasing fit of their hats. I think of all the autumns wasted, between my own childhood and now. All the collecting I forgot to do.

When there's a scuffle in the trees above us my small girl grabs my hand.
She points and looks up.
—Mummy, monkey!
—Oh, I say. Could it have been a squirrel, maybe?
She sighs, exasperated with having to explain everything to me.
—No Mummy, it's a monkey. I know. I seen it.
So we crouch next to the tree to get a better view of the monkeys, shading our eyes. Looking back along the path to wave to the others, dawdling towards us on the footpath, filling their pockets with acorns.

small

Three years in and I am still knocked off balance by the intensity of this love, by their relentless energy, by the magic of their conversations. With each new iteration I admire the people they are becoming and miss the people they have been. Each milestone of childhood, each gain, is also a parting from the previous version. I had not expected to learn so much about dinosaurs, or that shoelaces might be sea snakes and milk bottle tops are really biscuits for dolls. I had hardly noticed a thing about the world until now.

At three and a half, the past suddenly exists to them. Their own beginning their favourite story.
—I was in Mummy's tummy.
—And I was in Mama's, they like to say.
Fighting for some independent ground.
                                    I make the correction, a small edit.
—Not quite, I say. You were both in Mama's tummy, together, before you were born.
        —But you started in my tummy, before you were babies. When you were just tiny eggs.
—How tiny were we?
A favourite game, the list more extravagant each time
            —as small as an ant?
            —as small as a crumb?
            —as small as a Borrower's shoe?
—Smaller, I say. Smaller than all of those.
—I remember, she says. We were super small then, weren't we?

They bring it up, from time to time, over breakfast cereal or driving home from the shops.

The fairytale they star in. Heroes of their own creation.

Each time, a few more questions. Points of clarification.

Each time they ask, I tell it again.

An origin story of purpose and precision.

We wanted you, we made you.

A small dishonesty. Or maybe, something just right. A story abridged and edited for children.

—Were you lonely without us? They ask.

　　—Did you miss us before we were born?

◉

I don't tell them about the conversation that changed it all, five, six, years ago. We went to the sea to talk about it, some discussions are too big to have at your kitchen table. A weekend away, from work, from real life. A memory I play back on a loop, Beth and I, walking away from the hotel, until England runs out, country lanes becoming salt marshes and wide sky. A place empty enough for us to finally say the things we had been swelling with for years. We sit in the sand dunes and drink takeaway coffee, listing our options out loud. The pros and cons of changing our plans. A giving up or letting go. A shift. A turning point. All the things that might or might not be if Beth becomes the birth mother of our children.

Instead.

small

And maybe you could say it's no big deal. Luck not tragedy.
An unfair advantage, even, to have two wombs to try.

When we'd discussed this change of roles with the counsellor,
just a possibility, a Plan B, she had warned against it. Other
couples she had worked with had fallen for this temptation.
—Think of all the jealousy, she had said. The resentment.
—How could anyone bear it? The pregnancy you had dreamed of
        for so long, right there in your house, in your bed, but not
        in your body.

When the coffee is finished I use the cup to scoop up sand but it's
too dry to build castles. I pour out little mounds, dunes on dunes,
and remember from biology class that a cup can hold two million
grains of sand, a girl is born with one million eggs.
And if we don't change our plans?
If I keep trying to get pregnant,

                                she is frightened it will kill me.
                I am frightened she will leave.
If we do,

                she is worried it will break my heart.
                Or send me mad.

                                I am worried she is right.

                                ®

The summer I was pregnant with Beth's baby, I took it to work each day, buried inside me like a secret pearl.

❦

A positive test is a happy ending. The end of injections and tablets and scans. The end of intravenous transfusions and womb scraping and tube flushing. Years and years of scans and checks. Bruises to the skin and soul. An end to the psychological torture of knowing that, each time an embryo is placed inside you, you are pregnant until proven otherwise. Schrödinger's baby. A positive test to erase it all, all the years of failure, forgotten, because there was success in the end.

❦

I can hardly believe she was me. That poor woman. Laying on our bed, listening to the birds hopscotching on the guttering above the window as the nurse on the phone read back her date of birth and address, then, I'm going to put you through to the doctor now. Hold on. The doctor who asked the woman to rate her pain on a scale of one to ten. The doctor who told her to collect the blood in an old ice-cream tub. The woman who could not, of all things, bring herself to do that.

Two days later, at the clinic, Beth went in before me, catching the nurse before she offered her congratulations, I didn't need

133

them now. They gave me a print-out of the scan. The facts in black and white. **Products of conception.** Maternal age. I used the calculator on my phone to work out the exact length of my motherhood in weeks, days, hours, minutes.

I realized that July that I had misunderstood, all my life, what people meant when they said they couldn't sleep.
I'd had what I thought of as sleepless nights, airless summer nights before a storm, nights unsettled by the thought of an exam in the morning. I learned that summer what it was to not sleep because you are no longer able to. My brain never quiet enough to stop hearing the sound of it, water on water. I had never imagined there would be so much so soon. The unmistakable finality of it. Instead, I spend my nights at my desk, reading endless articles on the *mizuko kuyō*, the Japanese ceremony to mark and mourn the small lives of 'water babies'. The miscarried, the aborted, the stillborn. In the glow of my computer screen I visit the temples, admiring the blossom and jars of neatly arranged flowers, wondering about the plastic windmills. I understand these shrines. A place to grieve, to acknowledge, to remember. So I go there, scrolling numbly through images of toddler-sized Jizō statues in their red crocheted hats and capes, guiding the souls of babies never born.

◉

In a cafe near Regent's Park there is a waitress who lives in a
parallel universe.
Six years ago this July she offered me the blue-cheese special and
the gift of being able to decline it. An excuse to tell someone. And
of course I know that she forgot me instantly. And of course I
haven't been back since.
Congratulations, she said.

      Congratulations. How are you feeling?

                                            ®

I would like to forget that it happened in July.

                                            ®

And all I could say was sorry. Sorry. Sorry. I'm sorry I lost our
baby. And she would say, as she must, you've got nothing to be
sorry for. But I could not stop. Sorry. Sorry. Because there were
no other words to hand. No answers or excuses. It happens, the
doctor had said. Usually it is caused by an abnormality. The
chromosomes. Not meant to be.
An error then, I think, some small miscalculation, a stray digit in
the wrong column. Sorry.
Although maybe I meant sorrow. Sorrow. Sorrow. Sorry. Sorry.
Until she begs me, please stop. Please.
But I am just so sorry, baby.

small

I am so sorry I could not do what you needed or be what you needed.
A failure, a fault, an apology.
Sorry.

Sorry.

◉

None of this is in the stories we tell the children about their beginnings. It is not their duty to live knowing how much we fought for them.

It was not lightly done, I will tell them that. In time.
     About this.
     And the others.
     All those tiny lost lives.
     They were all real to us, don't think otherwise.
     Those tiny prologues of people, cells that cleaved and
     sparked, a beginning,
just,
but not enough.
It was not for want of trying. It was not for want of wanting.

In the years I was trying to get pregnant I painted the house from top to bottom. With all the zeal of first-time homeowners we stripped off generations of old wallpaper, repaired and painted the walls, the ceilings, the skirting boards. I spent a weekend painting the front door with endless thin coats of sage green. A whole month on the staircase, sanding, priming and painting each spindle in a smooth eggshell. Both types of painting did the job, hefty room renovations with ladders and rollers or fiddly projects only possible with a tiny brush. I had time on my hands I didn't want. Too much energy, too much time to think, too much out of my control.

There are so many small tasks in home renovations, so many seemingly crucial discussions to have over which kitchen tap to choose or which tiles would be best on the bathroom floor. The work was a diversion but also allowed us to imagine we were preparing the house, making it ready for a baby; really we were building a memorial to its absence. During the worst of it, I tore up the old carpet on the stairs in a fit of rage and grief. Hacking at the edges with a clawhammer and screwdriver I ripped up sheets of the stuff, pulled away rotting underlay, rusty treads and nails. The exposed raw floorboards were my penance to walk on for months.

When we moved from that house, two babies in tow, I shredded all the paperwork from the clinic. Moving was the perfect opportunity to destroy the evidence. The reams of prescriptions. Dates for scan appointments, blood test results. Lists of injections and schedules and well-laid plans. I threw out the letters from the doctor wishing us well. Better luck next time. The invoices for all that hope.

small

Credit cards maxed out on grief.
We had to book a large removal van to take all the cots, the toys,
the books. Our new family (instant, people said) outgrew the
home we had made for them quickly. Taking it over with all their
small things.

◉

I lie about it all the time, this truth my life pivots on.
People endure, more often than not.

Because of course I am ashamed of it, all that failure.
                    Ashamed of the size of my need.
        Such a small thing to want,
            two cells to meet and merge.
Years of effort trained on this microscopic thought.
Years lost to fruitless waiting.

                            Let it be forgotten.

◉

When we first shared the news that Beth was pregnant our
elderly neighbour had asked, over the fence, if we had tossed a
coin to decide who would carry the baby? My hairdresser told me
I had made a smart move. If she could have got someone else to
have the babies for her, she says, she *totally would have*. At work,
a colleague announces my arrival at a meeting with a jolly, 'Here

she comes, the woman who can't even be bothered to give birth
to her own children.'

⊛

How can I say that I would not want that baby now?
When its loss seemed to snap some vital thread in me.
Its small life was so hard won.
     Hers or
         His.
I do not want that baby now, nor any of the others that we made
and loved and lost so quietly.
     I cannot have both.
       Be both.

The truth is, there's no room in this house for dream babies, for
ghosts.
        All day long real children fill it.

And I am not discreet in my happiness.
I post photos of my children smiling,
I talk about them too much.
         Although I remember well enough.
         Although I promised myself I wouldn't,
         when I was on the other side.
     Living through the slow agony of it,
      left breathless by the stinging blows, the unexpected shock

small

of other people's happiness.
Arranging my face and adjusting my voice to meet somebody
else's good news.
As if their joy was a deliberate slight,
an insult.
An injury.
Congratulations! How do you feel?

Each time, telling myself it would be worth it,

in the end.
Each wedding toasted with sparkling water.
Each injection in a pub toilet.
Each credit card bill.
All the opportunities missed,
in the hope of crossing over from wanting to having,
from imagining to being.

The guilt of getting what you always wanted.

A traitor.

Life is only this.
Choices made and not made,
slips of judgement, unexpected chances taken.
There is no all to have.

◉

It comes, at last, one Sunday morning at the breakfast table, the
question I have been waiting for all this time.
—Why was Mama the one who got to have all the babies? My
        daughter asks me.
        —Was it because she's the bravest?
—Yes, I tell her. Yes. That is exactly it.

One day I will answer differently,
say more.

For now, I pay my debts to my daughters without speaking.
Because I did not grow your body inside mine,
I stay up for hours, sewing the torn seams of your favourite teddy
so you can wake up beside her.
Because I did not give birth to you,
I write your name in your new shoes in my best handwriting,
make your birthday cake.
Lift you on my shoulders.
Tuck you in at night.

◉

The background photo on my computer's desktop is one of my
favourites of Beth. Taken on that day, the huge sky and sea of the
Norfolk coast stretched in wide stripes behind her. A souvenir of

the conversation that made mothers of us both. The counsellor was wrong. I search for regret but I do not find it. I did not envy Beth during the pregnancy. I was not destroyed by grief. Love does not work like that.

In the photo Beth is leaning on one elbow in the dunes, the Marram grass around her swept left to right by the sea breeze. You can see from her outfit, a duffel coat, green scarf and sunglasses, that although it is a bright day it is not a warm one. The beach is beautiful and so is she. In the distance behind her a couple are walking on the same vast beach, deep in conversation, heads bowed, looking for shells or avoiding looking at each other.

It is a photograph full of big things. The sky. The sand. The back and forth of tides.

I keep it where I can see it, a record of the day I was finally able to stop trying to get pregnant, and start trying to be a mother.

One small change can change everything.

talk

She grows her best questions in a small silence.

A little trance of concentration,

                      then,

—If a crane lifted up our house, would there be loads of bugs
        underneath it?

I give it some thought.

                Our house, swinging at the end of a steel rope.

                  Pipes and wires dangling like roots.

The way insects scatter when a stone is moved.

—Yes, I say, as I lift her from the bath, as I wrap her in a towel.

      —I think there would be.

This is how we talk now.

Surreal fantasies built from half-heard words.

Phrases borrowed from cartoons,

           picture books,

                dreams.

The next morning, one of them tells me that the plums in the
fruit bowl can predict the future.

The other one can't get into bed that night because she needs a sip
of her potion first.

I don't contradict them.

                    Because they might be right.

Why not take a tip from the plums, there are worse ideas.

Far stranger than all of these fantasies are the facts fired across
the breakfast table.

small

—Did you know seahorses change colour when they are in love?
—Did you know that smells are made from atoms?
—Did you know that a blue whale's heart is the size of a car?

All day they come, these ambushing, disarming questions.
From the back seat of the car.
From pillows as they slide into sleep.

                                        Shy questions,
whispered in my ear each time I carry a small girl on my
shoulders.

                                        Awkward ones,
projected loudly, invariably in public toilets.
                              There are technical questions too,
reminders of all the things I have forgotten,
or never really knew in the first place.
I learn to mutter something plausible,
an overview of the water cycle, some bullet points on volcanoes,
playing for time until I can sneak off to Google it.
              The size of the moon.

                                        How cars work.

      Why trees have leaves.

The children don't ask me questions because they want to hear
my answers,
they ask because they want to explain to me what they are
seeing.

They ask me what crying is for.

Why people have to die.

It is hard, this talk.
Hard not to laugh, when a small child tells you she can't eat her
sandwich, because tuna's not her style. Hard not to be knocked
off your feet when she says,
—Don't say goodnight. I never want to be parted from you.
It's hard not to be careless in what you say.

How you say it.
Everyone knows that the things we mean least,
words thrown away in anger and exhaustion,
become who we are too.

People like to say it, that all this talking was inevitable.

Women's work.
So many mothers and daughters in one house.
The midwife, on the day they were born, who shook her head and
laughed at the very idea.
How, she had wondered, would anyone get a word in edgeways.
As if talking is all we do.

The talk is beautiful.
Profound.
Nonsense.
The way they insist wood pigeons are called 'morning owls'.
That there are umbrellas for bad weather and sunbrellas for good.

And there are dramatic turns,
the conversations which catch me by surprise.
A child appearing at my knee as I fill the sink with water,
or beside the bed in the dark, waking me with an
important announcement.
—I have something I need to tell you.
Or, more alarmingly,
—There's good news and bad.
And each time I brace myself, expect a revelation.
Although the thing they need to tell me is, they can't find a shoe.
Although the good news is, they would like a biscuit, please.

And when we talk they call us by our new names.
A name to summon help. When a zip is stuck. When a puzzle
piece is lost. When a sister won't stop or won't listen or won't give
it back.

That small name, an alarm in the dark that brings me running.
Alerting me to a wet bed or a bad dream.

Babies everywhere are born with it,
the word already in their mouths.
Then they wait.
For the right moment.
Looking their mother in the eye.
And for the first time, naming her.
Making her real.

100 words for snow.
I had not expected it to matter.
This name. And sometimes it is too much.
The faith children have in such a small word.
Asking it for reassurance.

> Screaming it as an act of possession.

We become what they call us.

This is motherhood. A story sold to all women, whether or not
they want to buy it. And who would volunteer for the job if they
knew?
The impossibility of it.
Be the object of devotion.
Be the obstacle to rail against.
All at once.

So we live and talk as though it has always been this way.
The four of us.
All of that trouble so far behind us.

> The clinic.

> The injections.

The counsellor who had been so keen to remind us, that these are
the small words used by other families. This name, a name for
other women.

small

Leaning back in her chair to ask,
                    —But what will your baby call you?
                                As if that was what mattered.

                            ◉

In the quiet evening hours, we start to ask each other if this is it,
the right time.
Paddling in the shallows of the same conversation,
the possibility of another baby.
We list all the practicalities and call them problems.
We talk ourselves out of it. This, surely, is enough?
And how would we even find the time?
With everything else there is to do now?
All the work and the play. All the washing and talking.
Making the decision doesn't make a baby.
We talk of our friends, their own baby-making troubles.
All of it less straightforward than our biology textbooks led us to
believe.
                    Acupuncture and supplements.
                        Fucking because an alarm on your phone
                    says it's time.

Where would we find all the new hours we'd need
for waiting rooms
and blood tests
and appointments?

We make our babies second
by second.
Cell
by cell.

But talking conjures the baby into being. A brother who might
be. A sister with potential.

Just the idea of it is joyful.
Another chance to fall in love.

Just the idea of it is painful.
Something greedy.
A betrayal of all that we already have.

◉

In May the children begin a new project, luring a robin to be
their pet.
Perhaps because they have so much in common, the energy and
alertness that robins and very small girls share. They set a trap
outside, half a strawberry and a folded tea towel, and wait. All
that month, the girls leap up from the kitchen table every time
a robin is spotted in the garden. Both quite sure that, if they can
only keep still for long enough, one of the small birds will come
to them. They stand, statues, on the garden path and wait. Right
arms held out in the pose of falconers.

small

And it would be easy to laugh at them, to tell them that their plan
is flawed.
But I would quite like to hold a robin too, feel its paperclip
footsteps on the palm of my hand.

I change that summer, I feel it in the muscles around my eye, my
vision being re-tuned to a new currency, all the things they see.
All the things I have been overlooking for years.
Pigeon feathers,
                    twigs,
            plastic horses,
                            keyholes.
The best small things are the small things you find under a tree,
                            on the beach,
            or on the pavement.
            Things small enough to keep in your pocket, or hold tight
                    in a fist.
Because seeing the small thing is never enough,
                                    you must touch it,
        own it,
            taste it, ideally.
Gather the small things close. Curate them on the windowsill or
        under your pillow. **Look carefully.**
Notice. All the small things that matter most.

◉

The robin plan evolves. It is possible, the girls agree, that robins don't eat strawberries. We take a walk along our street to see if we can find some robin food on the grass verges, turning the stones to find worms and woodlice. We collect the bugs in a plastic lunchbox and the girls sprinkle handfuls of grass on top to make them feel more at home. It is only right that we treat them humanely, before feeding them alive to the birds.

On our way back to the house we stop to watch a butterfly, as it walks slowly along the vertical edge of a car's wing mirror. The girls tell me that butterflies are very shy. They don't like people looking at them, or talking about them, they say. It's why they fly away so quickly.

—If you get close to one, you have to lose your voice so you don't
        frighten them,

like this, my daughter says.

            And she lip-syncs whatever it is you would silently say in
                the presence of a butterfly.

Insects take growing up so seriously, I think. No wonder children are so drawn to them. Grasshoppers and dragonflies who grow out of themselves, starting all over again. Butterflies and bees, transforming completely, ridiculously even.

The outrageous difference between the young and old.

—I miss our butterflies, one of the children says, and all the way home they reminisce about the 'Grow Your Own Butterflies' kit, a prized gift from their last birthday. At first it had seemed an underwhelming present, a small fold-out net, a booklet, a sachet of sugar. Then the tub of caterpillars arrived through the post. How earnestly they took on the project. We all watched the caterpillars carefully, patiently, photographing and documenting each stage of growth and change. Complying with the endless requests to read the life cycle of a butterfly leaflet as a bedtime story. I had thought, until then, that caterpillars became butterflies by adding to themselves, somehow. Changing into a new costume with wings under the cover of a cocoon. I was more amazed than the children when I read in the booklet that a caterpillar does not so much rest in its chrysalis as melt, breaking down into a soup of cells before rearranging into a butterfly. When we released them, the butterflies paused on the children's palms, waiting for permission to fly away. Surprised, perhaps, by their new freedom, the first feeling of fresh air.

—Why couldn't we keep them? The children ask me.

—They were our pets, we loved them.

So I tell them, that you have to let things go, when they are ready.

®

It happens so much sooner than I was expecting, the small voice raised to fill the kitchen.

—I don't love you anymore. You're not my mummy.

Because we talk like this too.

No baby book will tell you that.

As soon as daughters learn to talk, they learn to argue with their mother.

Their mothers.

That's good. It's right.

It's hard.

All of this is just practice, I know that.
There is so much more talking to come.
I have been rehearsing some of our future conversations since
long before they were born.

Harder questions are coming.

Harder answers.

◉

Against all odds, a robin flies into the house. The bird hops
up the concrete steps, comes in through the open door, and
makes a feast from the crumbs under the kitchen table. I don't
know whether to shoo it out or take a photo. For a moment I do
nothing, stunned at the coincidence, wondering if the children's
efforts have actually paid off. I move, cautiously, around the table,
hoping I can stop the bird flying further into the house, or worse,
dashing its head against the window as it tries to escape.
As I take a single step towards it, the robin hops out, as calmly as
it had hopped in.

◉

Months pass between one conversation and the next.
Months where the imaginary baby gestates in our minds.

small

A baby, who might be the best, or could be the worst, of all ideas.
The children are capable of so much now, we say to each other.
We're past all the nappies and night feeds. The teething. It would
be insane to go back to all that sleeplessness now, all that laundry.
No, we say to each other, on nights like this.

                                                    Let's not.

Everything is as it should be.

                              Nobody is that lucky twice.
                    And on the other nights,

we say yes.
It'll be fine.

                    Of course it is the right time.

Because this time is different.
We know what to do.

Because this time is different.
The baby has already begun.
An embryo frozen in time.

                    Waiting to come home.

                              ⊛

So much about the clinic is unchanged.
We walk through the same imposing front door, see the same
grand staircase. The lobby is brighter than before, a fresh coat of
paint, paid for by happy families and broken hearts. Expensive

flowers obscure the receptionist's view, an art installation projects images of spring blossom and blue sky onto the bright white walls. Beth and I hold hands to steady ourselves but it isn't the same, the stakes have changed. Our happiness is elsewhere this morning, digging in a sandpit or building a papier-mâché castle. As we sit in the waiting room I realize, for the first time, that I am more worried about the treatment working than it not. More aware of what a new baby will mean for us. Or perhaps this just seems easier, disarmingly so. So much of the hard work is already done this time. There are no eggs to collect, no sperm donor to choose. We know that nothing in this process is guaranteed but there is, at least, the possibility of a baby already.

I look around the waiting room. Some of the people here are clearly new to this torture, sitting too upright on the leather sofas, ready to leap up when they are called by the nurse. Ready to leave this building as soon as they can. As we drove into the city that morning I'd asked Beth how many hours, did she think, we had spent in the clinic over those years? We couldn't work it out. Too many, anyway. So much lost time, waiting in this room, looking at these walls. Hours spent downstairs in the treatment rooms. Hoping for a cure. Praying for a miracle. Hours, walled inside a small curtained cubicle, the air in the room thick with desperation and blind optimism. The collective weight of everybody's belief.

But there are no marks for effort here.

Not everyone will leave with what they came for.

small

The cubicle curtains separate patients but it is a communal experience, concertina folds which make other patients invisible, but not inaudible.

I won't forget it.

The sound that woman made when the nurse said,

—I'm sorry, I'm so sorry. The doctor wasn't able to collect any
     eggs this time.

Women drunk on sedatives. Laughing, staggering, insisting they are fine to go home alone.

—Call me a taxi, please. I'm fine.

The creaking of women climbing on and off hospital trolleys, fidgeting, adjusting, rearranging the blue paper roll which serves as a sheet.

And beside each bed, the single chair,

for a supporter, husband, wife, lover, friend, witness.

                    All of the above.

The most important work of the clinic can't be seen,

        not by the patients,

                not by the naked eye.

Deep in the basement of the clinic, the embryologists do their fingertip work.

Skin hidden under latex gloves. Eyes down, seeing the world in microscopic detail.

Think of their steady hands at work.

Excellent at threading needles,

or painting replica models of the Battle of Waterloo.

Think of the weight of responsibility.
Never slipping on the disinfected floor.
Never sneezing at the wrong moment.
The restraint.
To say nothing of the paperwork.
The consequences of an error.
The pressure of babysitting these impossibly small, indescribably important cells.

And you do worry about them.
The little globes of hope.
Frozen in time.
Like fossils in reverse.
You never stop thinking about them.

          The not-yets.

         And the not-evers.

      The just-in-case eggs of the women who aren't ready.

         The last-chance embryos of the parents-to-be

                who waited too long.

Stacked together, in their icy honeycomb.
Cells in cells.

There is nothing small about it.
This tiny ball of cells.
The beginnings of a person who might be our next great love.

               Or.

Might be the baby who disrupts it all.

small

The grain of sand that tips the balance.
A break in the symmetry.

I thought of it, of him or her, each time my train passed
underneath this part of the city.
As I watched the tourists stepping off for the zoo, I would feel it,
tugging.
Some unfinished business.
A feeling of the gas left on.
So I sent it my thoughts,
a wisp of white smoke.
Sent through the sliding doors,
minding the gap, and up the staircase,
out of the station
to swirl along the smart Georgian streets.
A drop of maternal comfort.
In through the barred window of the basement lab,
        where the not-yet babies wait.

parts

Their toys are everywhere, or so it seems. It is far from unusual to stumble upon a tableau of small bears, camping on the landing, or a family of miniature dogs founding a school in the downstairs loo. This is a new way of playing, not just copying what they see around them at home, but creating whole new universes. I watch them, lost together for days in their complex, highly plotted sagas. The kind of play most adults can remember, but know they can never truly get back to. Too far away from the ability to let the real world recede, too little faith in their own imagination. The great tragedy of adulthood. I know I should be grateful for the peace when they occupy themselves like this, I should leave them be, I should take the chance to work, but the games are just too irresistible. I contrive to fold washing in the corner of the room, or find something to tidy outside the door, just to have a glimpse. To store up a memory of the two of them like this. I watch them leading an expedition, an unlikely alliance of horses and dinosaurs, to the edge of the sideboard, making camp on a perilous cliff edge. The yellow sofa becomes a sandy beach where toys take their holidays. The blue rug, so obviously the sea. I saw it start, this new type of play, one Saturday morning, the two of them kneeling at the coffee table. Heads bowed together, praying, or playing. I watched them bring it to life, an elaborate tale starring a set of plastic rabbits that had come free with a comic, a blue-haired doll won in a pass-the-parcel. I know that this magic will stop, as quickly as it came. A last day will come as unexpectedly as the first, when one of them will grow out of playing like this, become self-conscious, more interested in the real world. Break her sister's heart. But for now, they live as much in those worlds as this. I see how much of a strain it is to drag them back to reality, to pull them out of a game to eat lunch or go to bed. These games that are lessons in negotiation. Experiments in ethics. Sometimes, they let a dinosaur fall off of the sideboard cliff and into the rug-sea. Sometimes, it takes the horses quite a while to mount a rescue. I watch them, playing with their power, because small is always relative.

Even small people have power over things that are smaller still.

Still, I am exhausted by the chaos of the toys, the avalanches of Lego bricks that settle on the carpet, the gruesome tangle of fake hair and plastic limbs when I open the cupboard door. So, periodically, I threaten to throw them all away. Dramatically dangling some unsuspecting princess over the bin to make my point. As if they were just pieces of plastic. As if they did not have my children's souls poured into them.

Afterwards, I sit alone in the kitchen, scrolling through the news on my phone. Quietly whipping myself with guilt, knowing I should know better. If nothing else, it is unreasonable to take against this one particular mess in a house full of so many others. What harm are the toys doing? It would be far more effective to throw the sink full of dirty dishes into the bin, or sweep the table top of unfolded laundry out into the street. As I scroll, my thumb teaches me a lesson, leading me to a news article on refugee children. Children finding a way to play, regardless. I click on

the first photo, a small Kurdish girl, sitting cross-legged outside
her family's tent in a camp in Turkey. In her arms sleeps a knitted
rabbit, wrapped tightly in a dirty towel, her fingers gripping onto
him with such love. I wonder what she has named him. I scroll
down. A boy, running a small toy car along a kerb in Calais. An
older girl, nine maybe, gripping a Bart Simpson doll as she sits
on the tarmac of a Greek port. The seam that is supposed make
Bart's hair spiky is unravelling. His eyes bulge in disbelief. He has
come a long way too.

Children always find toys, they make them if they have to, they
make do. Lucky children are given them, as Christmas gifts
and birthdays presents, hand-me-downs and raffle prizes. I lose
track of all the ways small toys breach the borders of our home.
An infestation of them. And some of the toys are immediately
forgotten, meaningless things. And some of the toys are loved to
destruction. Cloth teddies cuddled to shreds, dolls brushed to
baldness.

Each evening I scoop the invincible small plastic things into tubs
and I think about what it must be like for the men and women
who make them. How strange it must be to spend your day on
the assembly line that made this pearlescent plastic snowman,
these absurdly small doll's roller-skates. Stranger still, of course,
to pretend you don't know they were probably made by a child.

◉

small

We arrive far too early for the appointment so decide to walk
the long way to the clinic, past the gardeners circling the park on
ride-on mowers, past the queues of buses, the builders starting
work. It feels like an outing, a day trip away from real life. The
morning sunshine, the rarity of time like this, just the two of us.
We buy coffee to walk with and we don't talk. The talking part
is done. We don't talk about what will happen if it doesn't work.
We don't say to each other that, surely, we have started something
now that we cannot finish here. That this one chance would
never be enough. That there will, almost certainly, be more days
like this. More testing and scanning and injecting and waiting.
Moving backwards. We don't say it because we both know that
this is not about any cluster of cells. We have come to collect this
baby, not any baby.
This baby who began on the same day as the others,
triplets separated by time.

In the treatment room Beth and I hold hands, both watching
the screen of the ultrasound machine as the doctor prepares
to transfer our one thawed embryo. The embryologist comes
in, bearing our hopes in a thin plastic straw, and we all watch
the screen as the white line progresses, charting its course. The
catheter seems to turn, a right angle, once and then twice, as if
walking up a step and the doctor says
—There, you see, we just had a little mountain to climb.

Back in our cubicle, Beth rests, and the nurse comes in with a
print-out from the ultrasound.
The earliest of scan pictures.
—To pin on the fridge, she says.
I look at it, the bright white dash that I know is the embryo,
everything else around it a blur of black and white. A galaxy.

When we leave the clinic later that morning, Beth says,
—Let's not come here again.

details

Perhaps it is always different,

the second time.
The newness and sameness of pregnancy.
Beth grows the new baby casually,
an expert in her field.
There isn't time, this time,
to stop and moon over scan pictures.

But the baby grows.
Even if we hardly have time to notice it.
Or maybe all the noticing is Beth's.
Her waistband tightening.
Her nights earlier.
Full of the busyness of her body.

We don't read books or obsess over apps.
We don't sign up for classes or scroll through websites.
We've done this all before.
Twice.

At the twenty-week scan, the nurse says,
—At least you won't need to buy any new baby clothes.
And we drive home to tell our daughters about their little sister.

◉

small

All winter, Beth grows our baby.
The children snuggle in beside her on the sofa,
one

                    either

                                              side,

ears to the bump.
Fighting over who can hear the baby talking.
Who can feel her kicks and ripples against their cheek.
As the bump grow, so do their questions.

          Where will the baby sleep?
          What will she eat?
          Will she like dinosaurs?
          Will she have a twin?

The baby creates a new timeline, pulling us all towards early
spring.
Moving us towards a future when everything will change, again.

But I am pulled backwards to that winter,
back to the family I came from,
back to being a daughter not a mother.

                    My father's liver is failing.
                    For years he has been caught in cycles of it.
                              Illness, ambulance, intensive care.

But now, a lifeline has been offered, a place on the transplant
list. To prove he is a worthy candidate for the procedure the
hospital puts him through a series of physical and psychological

tests, finishing with a family workshop at the hospital. My mother invites me to come with them, as a note taker as much as a daughter. She is worried she won't catch it all, afraid she'll mishear some important detail. My father, too excited by this reprieve to write anything down.

They hold the transplant workshops somewhere in the attic of the hospital in a room designed for storage, not discussions of life and death. In the lull before things start, the families chat, hushed small talk to pass the time.

The good fortune of making that connection at Waterloo.

The story on the breakfast news about honeybees.

The weather much the same.

We sit in our rows of plastic chairs and size each other up. Smile-nod across the room at the people who are not quite strangers now. See, at a glance, which of them is dying.

A woman, about my age, holding hands with her husband.

A man in his twenties, all bones, sitting between his parents.

My father, the oldest among them.

We laugh, when the woman in front turns to ask,

—Is this your first transplant?

And stop when she holds up two fingers and a thumb.

Third time lucky.

The workshop is the last test patients have to pass to make it onto the liver transplant list. After the blood tests, the biopsies and CT scans, after the assessments by psychologists and social workers. The workshop is an education, or something else, a

small

lengthy disclaimer. You can't say you didn't know what you were
getting yourself into.
A nurse comes to the front of the room and opens a laptop.
We turn off our phones, arrange coats on the backs of chairs.

We are ready to listen.

Ready to wait.

◉

There are two waiting lists for transplant patients, the super
urgent and the chronic.
People die waiting, you know that.
An algorithm does the matching now, linking donor and
recipient on a database.
The computer decides: who is most suitable, who is most likely to
benefit.

Patients matched by age,
cause of death,
BMI,
blood group.
Sodium,
potassium.
good sense of humour,
kind to animals,
enjoys cinema and country walks.

The hospital calls it a Consent Clinic, but really it's a biology lesson. The nurse's presentation shows us diagrams of valves, pictures of organs, gruesome and beautiful. Sometimes, she issues a warning before clicking the mouse. The next image, she says, coyly, isn't so nice. On the left-hand side of the screen, a healthy liver, a shiny brown porpoise of a thing. On the right, its evil twin, warty and cirrhotic. She's right, it's not that nice. The nurse clicks the mouse again and the livers are whisked away. The next slide has a photograph of a sunrise. It's important, the nurse explains, pointing to the screen behind her, to maintain 'a positive attitude'.

We learn things.

> A 70kg patient needs a 700g liver.
>
> Large livers are ideal, the surgeon can divide them up and help two patients.

There is something comforting about the nurse, she is straightforward, bored even, by the miracle of moving a major organ from one body to another. All of it no more remarkable than fitting a new battery in a car. When she describes the equipment on the intensive care ward her accent turns machinery into missionaries. The missionaries that will help him breathe. The missionaries that will check his heart is still beating.

Being on the organ transplant waiting list is like believing in soul mates. Whatever the odds, you have to cling to the idea that that one special someone is out there, just for you.

small

When the nurse shows us a bullet point list of the signs of liver
failure, the atmosphere relaxes. This is our collective specialist
subject. The patients shrug, they know that their arms and legs
itch when bile collects under their skin. They smile knowingly
at ascites and muscle loss and insomnia. They know all about
asterixis, hands that flap and fly with minds of their own. Wild
birds at your wrists.

She clicks the mouse; encephalopathy has its own slide because
a poisoned liver doesn't contain itself, it infiltrates the blood and
that means the brain. Starting with a sort of foggy confusion,
growing into fits, then, if you're lucky,
just a coma.

And as the patients nod the relatives begin to fidget. Squirming
in our plastic chairs at the directness of it all. It is indecent,
somehow, talking about incisions and sutures, as if the diagrams
on the screen won't become the bodies of the people we love.
I feel my organs, twitching, reminding me they are working.
Absorbing, filtering, synthesizsing.
The telltale liver.

Just before lunch, the nurse hands round a bundle of plastic
tubes, a macabre quiz. The idea, she says, is to make the
strangeness of the intensive care ward familiar to us. Reduce the
shock.

This one will be down his throat,
this one will monitor blood gases,
this one will drain the wound,
this one will trickle liquid food through the nose to the stomach,
this one will be stitched under the clavicle.
I am grateful that she spares us the corrugated one they drain the
bowel with.

All of the workshop activities have a practical purpose. We need
to know what to expect because relatives are often required in
the hospital when a transplant patient is brought round from
anaesthesia. The high steroid dose makes them hallucinate,
panic, tear at all the tubes keeping them alive.
A familiar face, the nurse says, is a comfort.

◉

The final bullet point on the list of side effects for a liver
transplant is:

• death.

After you've had a liver transplant you can never eat grapefruit
again.

◉

Walking home from the station, I try not to look at the cars

parked outside the big houses. Liver transplant surgeons make
one vertical and two diagonal incisions on the patient's abdomen.
They call it the Mercedes scar. And of course I Google it as soon
as I get home. To see for myself. The red offal.
The yellow skin, pulled taut by metal paddles.
The accompanying words, softening the blow:
—During the operation, the surgeon will make a large cut across
     your tummy.

When I pick the children up from nursery that afternoon they
want to talk about the baby again. How did she get into Mama's
tummy? And their favourite topic, how will she get out?
—There are different ways, I tell them. But our baby will come
     out the same way you did, the doctor will make a small cut
     on Mama's tummy.

◦

In the days after the transplant workshop, time changes.
Fifteen minutes they give you, to answer the phone.
If you don't answer, the nurse moves on.
If you don't answer, the liver goes to the next person on the list.
Both my parents buy new mobile phones, as if the old ones won't
manage a call of this importance.
My dad moves the landline next to his bed; there won't be time to
find slippers, grope for the bannister, when the call comes.

We watch him settle to quiet readiness,
trying to think of other things.
Carrying on.
Checking his mobile when he thinks no one is looking.
A new habit,

a compulsion,
a religious observance.
A lifeline.
What else could you do?
Stay healthy, the leaflets say.
Eat well and 'relax'. Don't count the hours passing.

Waking up each morning, wondering if this is the day,
your mind a montage of flying calendar pages.
A showreel of Christmas trees,
birthday candles,
spinning hands on a clock face.
So he lives like a baby, eating and napping.
Waiting to transform.

⊛

At Christmas, Beth and my father sit beside each other at the
table, absurd opposites. He is shockingly thin and frail. She
shines, full up with the baby, of all the good things to come. It
would be hard to watch him like this, wasting away, if it wasn't
for the fact that we can all see he is so much better than he has

been for such a long time. An operation like this isn't wasted on lost causes. Looking at them side-by-side like this reminds me of it, the day my mother called from the hospital, telling me to come now, to be ready. How I had pushed the double pushchair, too fast, through the hospital corridors to find my father in the corner of a ward. A distortion of himself. His torso an egg, sticks for limbs, like a child's drawing.

The nurse looking after him couldn't resist the joke.

—Congratulations, sir! She said, tapping his huge stomach.

 I think it might be triplets!

It would have been an appalling thing to say, if it wasn't so accurate.

An old man's body, with a curved pregnant belly, smooth and hard. When the doctor examined him my father winced with the weight of it, the swollen middle tipping his centre of gravity, straining his back. My mum and I bounced the babies on our laps, arranging our chairs on the far side of his bed to keep it out of sight. The litres and litres of amber fluid they pumped out of him.

Liquid irony.

When the nurse returned with medication we all laughed again. All those years of swallowing to bring him here and he still couldn't manage to take a pill.

The liver has so many jobs to do, detoxifying, metabolizing, regulating, five hundred other things.

No machine can replace it when it goes wrong. Your liver doesn't care if you are profoundly sad, or perpetually lonely. It doesn't care if your addiction is a cry for help, or the result of a faulty gene, or a hairline crack in your character.

It does know every small sip you send it.

Miniatures lurking in the toilet cistern.

Half-bottles hidden behind the guest towels.

Glass skeletons in every cupboard.

❦

In the New Year I bring the baby clothes down from the loft and we sort them into piles to wash and fold. Everything is a memory. The inconceivably tiny vests the girls wore in the NICU, the hats that look like they would barely fit an orange. We unwrap all the sentimental things that have been neatly folded in vacuum-packed bags. The matching embroidered dresses the children wore to our friends' wedding. The surfer sweatshirts sent from friends in Australia. Soft pink cardigans knitted by my grandmother's friends.

Beth and I pass the clothes back and forth. Do you remember her wearing this one? I'd forgotten all about these. All the small clothes, clothes we changed and washed and changed again. Tiny outfits we wrangled them in and out of, at the side of a swimming pool, or at the doctor's surgery for check-ups and injections. Clothes we stripped off and buttoned on in the back of the car, in the toilets of a service station. These are the heroic clothes that survived the long days and nights of baby twins. The clothes that came off and on again when collars were damp with teething dribble, necklines yellowed with milky stains. It is a miracle, we say to each other, that this much survived. That first year when our washing machine was always running. But there are clothes which didn't make it to the afterlife of the loft, so many white vests and pyjamas lost on the front line.

The children are amazed by their baby clothes, and confused. We all marvel at them, how implausible it is that any of us were ever small enough to fit our limbs into these sleeves or necks into these collars.
I hold up two tiny pairs of trousers, jungle print with cartoon monkeys swinging around the knees.
—You wore these when you were babies, I say, setting them off on
    a spiral of questions.
—Were you a baby, Mummy?
—Yes, I tell them.
—How about you, Mama?
—Yes, Beth confirms. I was a baby once too.
—What about Grandad? Yes, we say, even Grandad was once
    this small.

cut

It almost always comes at night, the call to say that a stranger has
died for you.
Managing your tone of voice is the hardest part.
—Thank you, my father says, to the nurse who calls with the
        good news.

                                        If you can really call it that.

When the call is over he waits again,
as he has waited all this time.
Waited for his luck to change.
Waited for a miracle,
in a bed or on a list.
Now he waits by the door,
a man in labour.
Clutching his overnight bag,
waiting for the ambulance to bring him in.

The paramedics say blue light as if it is a verb.
—Don't worry, the younger one says,
        —we'll blue light you all the way there.
And they do, flashing along the motorway at speed.
        An emergency.
        The paramedics watch the road,

                                        and the clock.
My parents watch the city through the tinted windows, sleeping
office blocks and unlit houses.
Three quarters of an hour to think about it.

small

The other ambulance.
The other person.

At the hospital they prepare him. More blood tests, final scans, his skin scrubbed clean with antibacterial soap. Because getting the call isn't the end of things. Sometimes the liver isn't suitable after all. Sometimes it's a perfect match, but doesn't make it through the traffic, or the weather, or who knows what, to get to the hospital in time. Sometimes the operation doesn't go to plan. It's better to have a damaged liver than no liver at all.

His surgery begins at lunchtime. My mum sends a message from the train to say she is going home to sleep. She may as well, the operation will take the best part of a day, eight, maybe twelve hours. Don't call us, the hospital says, we'll call you.

There is nothing to be done that day, but hope.
That the surgeons aren't too tired,
that their fingertips don't slip.

                    Miss a connection.
        Drop a stitch.

Sixty years of small surgical discoveries, each improved method building upon the last.
Each new understanding a small change that makes the unimaginable possible.

And although it is the worst thing I could do that day, I spend
hours watching online videos of liver transplants. I study the men
and women in their surgical loupes – the glasses doctors wear
to magnify empty veins – pinching and lifting them with their
long, elegant tweezers.
I watch the surgeons flush and cut and stitch,
because the more I watch, the less I feel it.
The blood on blue gloves, just colours.
The stainless-steel instruments, just tools with stern names.

> DeBakey Tissue Forceps.
> Glover Bulldog Clamp.
> Berry Sternal Wire Twister.
> Satinsky Scissors.
> Langenbeck Retractor.

And as I watch, I wonder if I will get the chance to tell him
that these surgeons at their careful work remind me of him, no
different really to his head bent over a fuse box, the intricacy and
power of cables and electrical currents, held in his hands.

> The same head torch.
> Different tools.
> Mole grip.
> Screwdriver.
> Wire cutters.

◉

small

I fall asleep that night thinking of the new liver,
settling into place under his rib cage,
        making itself at home.
This new living thing.
        Hoping for acceptance.
                Trying to fit in.

My father sleeps that night.
Deeply.
Chemically.
Machines pumping air into his lungs.
Tubes and drugs attending to their duties.
And as he sleeps, the rest of us wait,
to see if his body has noticed yet.
This stranger.
                A foreign body it might attack.

                                        Reject.

He doesn't think at all,
far away from consciousness.
All that he doesn't know not hurting him.

But not everybody waits patiently that night.

Five weeks ahead of schedule, with a gush of water that floods
our bed,
our unborn daughter announces her imminent arrival.

My mother dresses in the dark, again.
And as she drives to our house, she wonders,
if all her nights will be like this now.

     Phone calls.

          Emergencies.

               Hospitals.

She makes herself a cup of tea,
a bed on our sofa,

                                    and waits.

For the phone to ring, again.

     For a child to wake,

          small footsteps on the stair carpet.
Padding into the room to ask impossible questions.
—Where is everyone, Nanny?

     —What's happening?

And it snows.
Of course it does.
The first of the year and the roads not yet gritted.
Six inches deep by the time we arrive at the hospital.
I guess at where a parking space might be and help Beth out of
the car.

◉

small

I am grateful for the bad weather that night, it gives me
something to do.
The nurse tells Beth to rest.
—Just wait, she says. Save your energy for tomorrow.
But it is easier said than done on an uncomfortable hospital bed,
on wet sheets.
I watch the snow.

Gathering on the window frames.

Falling.

Wait, until morning, the nurses keep telling her.
It's better to have a baby in the daytime.
Doctors back on shift.
Daylight.
Everything will be different then.
Easier.

From my chair in the corner of the room I watch Beth chasing
sleep. Trying to find an arrangement of back and bump in which
she can rest.
—It's all very well, she says, to tell me to wait. But who's to say
        that this impatient baby will listen?
When she can't sleep, we talk, joke that this is our first night away
from the children in years, an unlikely romantic break. But we
aren't alone. Her presence fills the room already.
This small person we're waiting to meet.

At about five in the morning the hospital wakes up. The sounds of cleaners, moving through the corridors, polishing the floors to a shine. Cars creeping through the slush of overnight snow. One possible birthday has come and gone. The impatient baby misses Imbolc, the first day of February, the start of spring. The sign of all the light that is to come. As the new day and the new season edge in, Beth finds some sleep at last. I find a pen at the bottom of my bag and make notes on the back of an old receipt, middle names that mean snow.

®

The doctors arrive in the early morning, smelling of coffee and toothpaste. They perform an ultrasound scan to check the baby's size and position. They frown together at charts and discuss the various options, deciding, in the end, to come round to the baby's way of thinking, it is the right time to be born. Beth is admitted to the prenatal ward and told to prepare for a Caesarean. When the surgeon and anaesthetist come to speak to her they joke that she is a professional at this now, reading aloud from her notes that she is an authority, a 'mum to the power of two'. Beth is business-like this time, she wants the project completed, wants to get out of here, back to real life as quickly as possible. If she's worried she doesn't show it.

I go out into the car park to call home, walking gingerly on the pathways, slick and sparkling with frost. The girls are fine,

my mother says, we exchange hospital dispatches. I tell her the
Caesarean will be today, we think, maybe early afternoon. She
tells me he hasn't come round yet but was stable overnight. When
he wakes up, we say, he'll have a new granddaughter, won't that
be better than a bunch of grapes? We agree to text if there is any
more news, from either hospital. Before I hang up the girls take
turns to come on the phone. They ask me when we're coming
home as if we have been lost to them for weeks.
—Soon, I say. We'll all be home soon.
Back on the ward I pack Beth's things into the overnight bag
so we're ready to move when the call comes. I fold her spare
nightclothes, underwear, the new slippers bought just for the
hospital. I pack and re-pack the baby's tiny nappies, Beth's wash
bag, her earphones. Around midday the midwife on duty comes
to let us know it's time to get ready, and looks me up and down.
—What size jeans are you wearing? She asks, realizing, just

      in time, that the scrubs they keep for fathers to wear in the
      operating theatre will be far too big.

She returns, minutes later, after a raid on the staffroom lockers,
presenting me with a set of the nurses' spares.

In the final hour before the operation I lay out our daughter's
first outfit. Something brand new before her life of hand-me-
downs begins, an all-in-one suit in a soft cream fabric, a friendly
fox stitched across the front. We know that she is likely to be
too small for it so, just in case, I arrange a little pile of her sisters'
old things too. The doll-sized vests and suits they had worn, just

a corridor away from here, on the NICU. When the midwife comes to fetch us for the operating theatre she tells me to wait.
—Don't forget this, she says, placing a small woollen hat in the cot. I knit them for all my babies.

Before the surgery begins Beth mentions she feels nauseous so the anaesthetist puts an extra cannula in the back of her right hand. He inserts the needle too quickly and sprays us both with her blood. A nurse wipes the blood from Beth's arm and face and the midwife leads me into the scrub room to show me how to clean my hands and arms before I'm allowed back into the operating theatre.
—It'll be fine, she says. Just don't touch anything blue.
I'm grateful for the clear instruction, something achievable at last.

There is something unreal about the birth. The exact same room, the exact same surgeon, asking Beth if she can feel anything as she draws the scalpel across her middle, a thin shallow scratch to start, just to be sure. I sit, as before, by her side, holding her hand, holding her gaze. But this will be nothing like that day. A routine procedure by comparison. Just one baby. Already bigger than either of her sisters had been.

The medics take their register, introducing themselves, calling out their names and titles, revealing the people they are behind the masks and gowns.
I watch but don't touch them, these blue gods.

small

Theatre is still the right word for it.
                              The suspense.
          The intensity.
A theatre of comforting modernity.
                              Bright lights.
All the props in silver and surgical green.
          The medics chatter as they work, checking stats, the time,
          heart rates.
Marking out each step of their methodical and routine work.

And when it starts to go wrong it is not a surprise,
but somehow,

                              the thing I had expected all along.

She had been too easily won.
This baby who had waited so patiently on ice,
to be born so urgently in snow.

They cannot disguise it.
The change in atmosphere that colours the operating theatre.
The shift in volume, the tone of their voices.
Switching, as if we won't notice, to code words,
to meaningful eye contact.

And we can see how hard they are working, not guiding, but
pulling, at the baby.
One surgeon leaning back for ballast, the other straining at

Beth's body, stretching open a space for escape. I stand up and look over the sheet that is pinned from Beth's chest and see the baby, legs and body born, her head still trapped. A diver half submerged. Blue skinned.

—Enough, the midwife says. I'll do it if you won't.

And in a scuffle of disagreement with the scrub nurse she lifts a phone on the operating theatre wall and pages the emergency crash team.

holding

They take her to the Special Care Baby Unit,
to check.
The surgeons don't pause, shifting their attention back to Beth
and the layers of stitches they need to make. Meticulously
undoing all their hard work, they sew up all their careful
incisions, as if their knives had never been there at all.
Beth tells me to follow the baby and I race down the corridor
after her.
—Where do you think you're going in such a hurry? The midwife
        calls after me.
—With the baby, I say. It's ok, I know where the NICU ward is.
—Not dressed like that, you're not, she says. You'll have to get
        changed first.
Beth's small hospital room is suddenly too big, too empty
with no bed in it, no patient. I take off the scrubs as quickly as
I can, tangling myself in the legs, pulling on civilian clothes,
scrambling for my shoes under the wipe-clean chair. When I
burst out into the corridor I show myself to the midwife, my
hands in the air like a cornered prisoner, and she nods her assent
for me to leave.

I run after our baby and the strangers bearing her away from us.

I catch up with her in the room closest to the nurses' station.
The smell of alcohol from the hand gel, the beeping of heart-rate
monitors swimming around me as if minutes, not years, have
passed since I stood here last. The baby is flanked by guards. A

doctor, on her left, leans over her, listening to her tiny heart with
a stethoscope. A nurse, to her right, is frowning at a clipboard.
—Are they sure about this weight? The nurse asks. It's unusual
for a baby this premature, I would expect her to be much smaller.
I'll ring down to theatre to check they've written it down
properly. The doctor's pager buzzes at her waistband; excuse me,
she says, I'll be back in a moment.

And they both leave.

I am alone with her.

In a room no more than three metres square.

Walls lined with neat plastic drawers, full of tiny needles,
syringes, vials. All the essentials of hospital work, shrunk down
to neonatal size. Above her cot, hanging from the surgical light,
is a small mobile. Three plastic sheep, a moon, a star. A small
concession to babyhood.

The nurse has wrapped the baby in tight layers.

Blanket,

towel,

blanket.

On her head she wears the midwife's hand-knitted hat,
its chaotic mixture of yellow, green and fuchsia wool.
I rest my hand, gently, on her chest and whisper a hello.

Our first touch.

Fingertips to heart.

She gets the hiccups, tiny squeaking jolts in her sleep.
I take my phone from my jeans pocket and film it so Beth won't
miss a thing.

Then, I take a photo of her, minutes old.

Eyes closed, her face not yet fully cleaned from birth.

I send the picture to my brother.

—Can you show this to Dad? I say.

    —When he wakes up.

If.

The doctor and nurse come back into the room and I reposition myself at the end of the cot so they have space to work. I watch as they check the tone of her muscles, watch them insert the tap in the back of her soft new hand to collect blood samples. Through it all, she sleeps, and sucks her thumb, as if it is no trouble at all, to be poked and prodded like this in your first hour in this world.

—Does she have a name? The doctor asks.

And when I tell her she says,

—Lovely.

    —As in the small bird, or the French city?

—The bird, I say.

When they are satisfied with their checks, the baby is placed in a Perspex cot on wheels, her notes slotted into a built-in folder at one end. The nurse tells me I'm allowed to push the cot myself, if I'm careful, and we set off in a procession along the hospital corridors to deliver her back to Beth. We find her, sitting up in bed, eating the regulation toast and tea, the meagre reward handed out to all those who perform the miracle of birth. Beth holds the baby into the snug of her neck and I feel myself breathe out for what feels like the first time.

®

And we might have stayed like that for hours, if we were allowed.
The three of us in our small hospital room, with nothing more to
do than look at each other.

Ignoring the shock of it all.
The unreality.
Until we start to test each other, both hesitating to be the one to
pose the halting questions.

Does she...

seem

ok,

to you?
Should we...

ask someone,

about the crash team?
Were they really needed?
Did the midwife overreact?

Did the surgeon make a mistake?

But there isn't time to ask a thing, the midwife is back in the
room, hurrying me into my coat and out of the door. Visiting
hours are about to finish, she says, you'll need to be quick if you
want to get those big sisters here today. So I leave this baby sooner
than I want to, just as I had left the others, kissing her knitted
head to drive home and bundle her big sisters into their car seats.
I steer them through the town, and back to the hospital car park,

without pausing. When we arrive I take a small hand in each
of mine and they walk their little skipping steps through the
automatic doors, waving at the nurses behind the desk.

—They're in here, I say. Mama and the baby, but let's be quiet, in
case they're sleeping.

But they aren't sleeping, in the half hour I have been away from
the hospital the midwife has improvised a party. On the bedside
locker she has set two plastic beakers of orange squash, decorated
with the girls' initials in permanent marker. Beside the drinks, a
paper plate of biscuits pilfered from the staff room. The midwife
knows how to work with three-year-old egos. She calls them big
girls and shows them how to take Beth's blood pressure. Then,
they take it in turns to sit on the hospital chair, holding their
hours-old sister on their laps. Oddly, it makes them seem smaller
again, the scale of the baby against them in this adult pose, their
soft hands cautiously wrapped around her. The midwife and I
taking turns to act as a safety barrier, holding the baby's weight,
supporting her soft new head.

The midwife takes photos, the five of us, grinning, in various
combinations. Through it all, the baby sleeps, then feeds a little,
then sleeps again. Her sisters crowd round her, reaching out to
touch her fluffy hair, squabbling over whose finger she likes to
hold best. What a gift it is for all of us, I think, to be able to say to
her, we have known you always, loved you since the day you were
born.

small

Before I take the girls home for their bath, the midwife says we can all come up to the postnatal ward to see where Beth and the baby will spend the night. So we pack up the bags once again and the girls are given important things to carry; the baby's hat, Mama's slippers. As we are about to leave she comes in waving a piece of paper.

—Good news, the midwife says. The blood test is back.

Then, in a matter-of-fact tone,

—It's fine, she says. Her brain wasn't starved of oxygen during the birth.

We hadn't even known they were testing.

®

Every few hours a nurse comes to draw a drop of blood from the baby's heel to check her bilirubin levels. Sometimes the blood flows easily. But too often the nurse is only able to raise a small dark bubble, squeezed from a reluctant tiny foot. She shakes her head and calls for the doctor.

—Jaundice, just a touch, the paediatrician says, very common in premature babies.

He prescribes light therapy and the nurse settles her under the blue lamp, carefully adjusting the eye mask that makes her look like a baby superhero. Beth and I sit beside her cot, drinking hospital coffee and reading the symptoms of jaundice on our phones, as she glows neon blue.

Her liver is too small, the websites say, not yet ready for its
lifetime of work.

In the end Beth and the baby spend a week in hospital, but it
is nothing like before. There are no wires, no breathing tubes.
During the night she sends me pictures, the baby on her lap,
eyes half-open, quizzical. The baby just back to sleep after a feed,
wrapped tightly in a swaddle, or layered in white waffle blankets.
The photos are blurry, taken in the dark of the hospital ward
at night, undercover shots of their secret life together. In the
daytime I send Beth pictures of the girls, backpacks on, heading
to nursery. Sitting at the kitchen table, chins and cheeks filthy
with pasta sauce.
Snapshots of what the other is missing.

I bring them both home on a Thursday afternoon and the five
of us have a party to celebrate, setting out the picnic rug on the
carpet and tying bunches of balloons to the furniture. We eat
iced biscuits and sausage rolls and the girls say it is a shame that
the baby can't eat yet, milk is not as nice as crisps.

⊛

My father meets the new baby when they are both freshly home
from hospital.
He holds her in two cupped hands and she sleeps.
We leave them for a while, retreating to the kitchen.

small

Everyone can see there is something shared between them,
something private,

                    these two new lives.

By April he is already stronger, taller somehow. His skin the
colour of skin again. His life changed. When he visits, he wears
a tweed cap as if, perhaps, dressing the part makes him feel like a
more qualified Grandad. He doesn't really have enough hair for a
game of hairdressers but the children persevere, forcing clips and
bows into his short white hair. What he lacks as a hairdresser's
client he makes up for as a compliant patient, allowing the small
doctors to bandage his knees and check his heart with their
plastic stethoscopes.
—There Grandad, my daughter says, with convincing authority.
—I am a doctor and you're not poorly any more.
When it is time for my parents to leave that day I cannot stop
myself.
—Call me, I say, so we know you got home safely.
Words of mundane comfort sent along the phone line.
The children run to the doorstep to hug him goodbye, clinging
to his legs, holding him tight,
willing him to stay.

                         ◉

There is another story but I don't know it.
Another family.

Another call that came in the middle of the night.
There was a person I don't know and can only imagine.
A person with their own love stories, and achievements,
their own bad habits and unfinished business.

A missing piece in a family.

®

We settle back into the chaos of newborn nights and days. We
don't open the baby books. We don't Google. Not once do we
rush the baby to the doctor fearing some rare illness.
She is fine and we trust ourselves.

She finds her place quickly too.
Watching us all from her bouncy chair, or peering out from a lap.
Waiting for her chance to join in.

It is fine, of course it is, shifting our lives to fit around a new baby.
Although they seem like different species.
Three-year-olds and newborns.
How impossible it seems that they were once like her.
And more unbelievable, the fact that she will be like them,

one day,

and soon.

Bouncing on beds and drawing faces on each other's knees.
Running and talking and changing faster than seems fair.
But for now,

small

I can bathe her in the bathroom sink.
Left arm holding her whole body, right arm scooping water over
her skin.
And each bath time, I wrap her in a towel and hold her up to the
mirror, her face beside mine.
Some foolish idea that I am taking our portrait, capturing this
moment of daily perfection.

Another day navigated.
A baby warm and clean.
A baby changed, imperceptibly, since yesterday.
It is risky, looking in the mirror like this.
Pausing to see her change, I see myself changing too.
Maybe the worst thing you can do to your children is look at
them too closely,
making them the beginning and the end of who you are.
    The time will come,
        one day,
            when they will want to look back at you too.
    To find a person, not just a parent.
**How do you make sure you'll still be there when they come to
find you?**

hours

Night, you call it, although the birds outside sound fairly sure
it's morning.

The baby, still waking, awake again.
   Bewildered mid-dream, her arms reaching up to you.
        The injustice of being left alone.

You try all the usual things,

          rocking,

      walking,

   singing,

             begging.
You work thorough the checklist of baby woes, trying to coax her
back to sleep.
You are the only two people awake in the whole world.
It's not the crying babies, but the sleeping ones, that break your
spirit. Crying babies are chemical reactions, milking you for
adrenaline, rage, self-pity. The real test comes on the nights you
find yourself trapped under the feather-weight of a baby curled in
sleep, afraid to move, breathing as quietly as you can to survive.
That's when you hear them. All the sounds of the night, the
crowbars prising open your kitchen window, the melody of all
your self-doubt ringing in your ears.

If it were a love affair you would leave it, this mess of power and
control you're caught up in. Sitting once more in the straight-
backed armchair, you think of all the hours you have spent like

small

this. This baby, the others. All the secrets you have stored in the curves of their tiny seashell ears. All of the impossible promises you have made.

The room is made strange by shadows. The folds of the curtain, the patterns on wallpaper, and all the things they turn into at night.

> Is this why the baby won't sleep?

®

It is only recently that we have thought of the night as one long stretch. Roman mothers had four small nights to get through before dawn, poor things. Each watch of the night counted out in water clocks, tired arms and heavy eyes. Nights that are sharp with loneliness. Nights that are full of all the people who have come before. All the other women who have stood in this old house before me, looking out of this window, a baby on her shoulder, longing for her bed.

These hours are not empty. The nights not free from adventure. You abridge the list to a highlight reel:

> The night you tripped on the stairs, spraying formula milk in an arc on the wall.
> The night you found, with horror, a slug on the kitchen work surface as you made up a bottle.
> The night you heard teenagers coming home as the night

tipped into light. Singing and pushing each other into the empty road.

All the nights that you and the baby have seen. All the nights you will remember, all the nights she won't, in this time before memory. All the small hours you have spent awake, and not. In that place where memories find you. Lurking. The names of friends from school, lost in time. Song lyrics you can't shake off. The memory of your brother's pet goldfish that everyone forgot to bury. Found years later in the garden shed, a skeleton in a matchbox.

And when she sleeps, her body resting on the slope of your chest, her head in the crook of your neck, then you think, surely, this has been well designed.

And when you sleep, finally, you find your sleep has changed. You sleep too close to the surface, alert and electric. Waking with a start, thinking you have smothered a baby. Digging at the covers, searching under pillows, until the voice beside you says Stop. A hand on your arm, pulling you back under the sheets. It's ok, she's safe in her cot, look. Look.

And, of course, you have been awake all night before, but not like this.

Not with so much at stake.
This is not the sleep you lost dancing, walking home in the grey

morning with your shoes in your hand.
These are not the nights you spent on gossip and movies either.
                                        These nights are the end of sleep.
The nights when you understand you will never sleep again, not
really.
Not now there are rivers and roads and diseases to worry about.
                                        The price you will pay.

◉

Nobody wants to hear about your sleepless nights, you are not
heroic – only tired.
Telling people about it is like talking about your dreams, or
describing how it feels to fall in love.
        Some things are lost in the telling.

◉

Only one thing comes to you with clarity on these nights. How
could you not be grateful? To think that someone once did this
for you too. Listened to you breathe. Held you when you called
out. Sat with you while you learned how to sleep.

◉

Morning always finds you. On the floor beside the cot, your
arm numb through the bars. On the sofa beside a bouncy chair.

Maybe, sometimes, even in your own bed. All the work of the
night just a warm up for the long day to fill, the weight of the
pram that needs pushing along the towpath to watch, again, the
changing of the guard, in the rain. The spy's view on the world
you are gifted when nobody notices you.

Or maybe, today is Tuesday and you can hide for a few hours
at a baby group with all the other women reduced to this from
former lives, elevated to this by their new name. Sitting on the
floor together, winding the bobbin, or rowing the boats. Songs to
drown out all the lives we had lived before this.

◉

The next night and the next night will be the same.
The bedtime routine stretching out.
Elaborate teeth-brushing rituals,
the sacred placement of twenty-five stuffed animals in the bed.
—Tell us a story from your mouth, they say, just as I think I can
          sneak out of the room.
The improvised bedtime stories, where it is implicit they are the
heroes.
Shrunk to the size of toys or possessed of magical powers.
Plots I borrow from films or fairy tales,
re-cast with a favourite aunt, an ice princess, a misunderstood tiger.
And later, I will stand at the ends of their beds, checking they
have remembered to breathe.

small

Listening to the whisper of it.
Just to be sure.
The older girls arranged in dramatic poses,
right arm flung across the forehead, left foot touching the floor.
The baby curled up, bottom in the air.
Isn't this the biggest night-time secret of them all? Nature's
greatest practical joke. After all the last long hours of the day,
when parents watch the clock, smooth out the frayed edges of
everyone's temper. When everyone in the house holds fast to the
rituals that will see you through. The warm bath, the cup of milk,
the story, then another story, then please just one more, then a
lullaby. The sweet sorrow of parting.
And then
when the day is over,

                    relief,

                         silence,

                                    hunger.

All the mess of the day,
       all the work not yet done.
                   And worst of all, absurdly, a homesickness.
The realization that you will never be hardened to it, their
absence once they fall asleep.

So, just for a moment, you sit at the top of the stairs, lost in the
screen of your phone, looking at photos from the day.

Checking over and over again that your life is real.
Your life is real.
It is real.

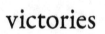

victories

Every Sunday night,
between bath time and bedtime,
the tiny moons of their fingernail clippings
gather in the sink.
Why not say it, when it's true?
There is poetry in all of these mundane intimacies.
Being responsible for someone else's ear wax is an act of love.

Caring for the children's bodies is work.
The long shifts of monitoring and sustaining them,
   making sure they are clean,
      and fed,
         and vaccinated.
All the checks and balances of it.

Does it go without saying that I am amazed by these small bodies?
All the things they can do.
      That they exist at all.
Why should you watch a body you once held in the palm of
your hand,
now riding a bike, or running through a sprinkler,
and pretend it is anything other than a miracle.
   Tiny cells replenishing.
     Soft bones stretching out.
     The pace of it,
forcing you to look,

small

more closely,
small bodies, growing before your eyes.

And there will be years of work ahead,
to keep the small bodies in working order.
The re-fuelling and wiping clean.
All the brushing and dressing.

                              But maintenance is the easy part.

Vigilance is the thing that turns your heart sideways in your
chest.

One eye always open,
        checking for rashes,
                        temperatures,

                                        pains.
Finding the thermometer,
measuring out the medicine.
Rolling a glass on the skin while praying.

Because even the closest surveillance can't stop them all.
The sore throats and earaches and tummy pains.
All the unseeable germs, passed between children,
like football stickers, or marbles.
        Scarlet fever.
        Chicken pox.
        Hand, foot and mouth disease.

The ailments of Victorian urchins.
Beloved small bodies, sweating and vomiting in the dark.
    Confused.
    Afraid of their weakness.

So you are there,
a bigger body, strong enough to lift theirs up,
to reassure.

Hands that will strip the bedsheets,
and run a midnight bath.
Find the clean pyjamas.

A comforting body that will stretch out on the carpet beside the
bed.
Keeping vigil.
Waiting to do it all again,
who knows how many times, before morning.
Not sleeping, but wondering.
Scrolling through the internet,
reading the names of all the rare things it might be.
Staring at the ceiling.
Counting all the pointless clichés of your emotions,
how quickly you would take their place,
all you would wager to make them feel better.
And you wait.
                    For morning.

small

For this to pass.

                For a return to unremarkable days.

Because these are the small victories which count now.
The sanctuary of predictability.
Days and days when everything is simply
                fine.

Things continue.
That's all you're really aiming for.
Food is bought and cooked and eaten.
                Children thrive.
This is winning now.
Language betrays you anyway.

                      This drowning,
in baskets of unmatched socks,
in the cardboard piled by the door, waiting to be recycled.
Drowning in the responsibility of each day.
All you can do is deny it.
                Stay afloat.
Tell everyone you were just waving, all along.

Because this is a life of endless small failures too.
Incomplete tasks.
Lists and lists of jobs that will never be done.
        The thin rim of limescale around the bath plughole.
        The back door keys, perpetually lost, in the absence of

time to screw a hook into the wall.
A cracked bathroom tile.
A curtainless window.
Pictures waiting years to be introduced to a wall.

And the jobs that you do unravel so quickly.
A newly painted wall, dappled with small fingerprints
within the hour.
A freshly made bed, just an invitation to start
trampolining.
When all the work of family life seems futile, Beth and I say to
each other, half-jokingly,
this is work fit for Sisyphus, for Hercules.
Elevating the blocked dishwasher to the stuff of legend.
Invoking some heroic pride as I stand, mop in hand,
surveying the kitchen floor,
a sea of crumbs and footprints to conquer.

And I carry on living like this as if I don't know any better.
As if I can't see pictures of perfect lives, right there in the palm of
my hand.
The monochrome playrooms and clean kitchen islands of other
families.
Screen after screen of how my life could look.
And when I look up from my phone I see instead,
baby photographs stuck to the fridge door.
Princess stickers permanently welded onto the backs of chairs.

small

Rows of drawings and paintings, pegged on string above the kitchen table,
a canopy of their imaginations above us as we eat.

> A rabbit on a motorbike.

> Two spiders made from paper plates.

> Assorted sea creatures.

> Rockets.

> Fossils.

◉

A change in the light makes it visible, a faint drawing, sketched in yellow felt-tipped pen. What appears to be a rectangular bodied lion with sharp claws, drawn directly onto the glass on a low corner of the kitchen window. Perhaps it has been there for weeks.

I round up the prime suspect and bring her to examine the evidence.

—Did you draw on this window? I ask.

She looks up at me, absorbs the question in silence, and thinks carefully.

—No, she says, I didn't.

I search her face for a tell. A twitching lip, a nervous blink.

—Are you sure? I say.

—I didn't draw on the window, she repeats.

A pause.

—But I did draw on that wall.

You have to admire it, the complex morality of small children.
The unrelenting sense of justice, even when it is misplaced.
As we talk, I try to unravel it,
the good thing that was telling the truth,
the bad thing that was drawing on the wall.
The mess I make of it all by admitting,
that, yes, they are both good drawings,
but, no, you shouldn't draw on windows or walls.

Children enjoy the clarity of rules, people say. They like catching
people breaking them.
Wielding the ultimate threat, the power to tell a grown-up,
bringing the full force of the law to punish your sister's crimes. At
the front of their minds, the children hold an ever-growing list of
things that cannot be tolerated:

      fighting,
      lying,
      stealing.
           A clear moral universe.

Smaller infringements, they start to learn, are best kept between
themselves.
Pushing and shoving that gives as good as it gets.
The cup they break together, the pieces they hide, together.
Learning the truth quickly, the grey areas are where all the living
really happens.

And I must be ready, to be the arbiter.

small

To have my own moral compass put to the test.
All the ways I profess to know what is right,
all the efforts I make to teach our children lessons in restraint,
patience,
tolerance.
Although I have let a wild scream of frustration fill the kitchen,
and watched their faces change.
Although I have held a small wrist, too tightly, as I marched a
screaming toddler from a shop.
Although I have been furious and tired and despairing,
on the very edge of my own control.
The shame and guilt of using your power,
the big over the small.

Because tantrums are two-sided things.
        Cause and effect.

                                        Performer and audience.
Normal, understandable, things.
Better to teach them honesty, name your angers, let them be seen,
I want to say.
And I think about how much I want them to embrace all
experience, feel pain openly and learn from it.
And I think about how much I want them to stop wailing in the
supermarket car park.
Tiptoe carefully, if you can, along this fine line.
                Let it be.
                Make it stop.

So we learn new ways to control ourselves.
New ways to look beyond the things that annoy and frustrate.
Knowing that all of this is inevitable.

The friction of being so close.
The strange power dynamics of a young family,
our interdependence,
the contradictions of it, remaining constant,
always changing.

And one of them controls herself too much.
Fixing her mouth in a smile, eyes big and wet,
swallowing, swallowing.
        Showing me what she thinks I want to see.
And the other rolls and sobs and pours out her tears at will,
        the smallest slight provoking grief.
Both of you are too far away from the middle, I think.
Don't cry so easily.
Don't wait so long to cry.
                But they are only beginners at living.
                They'll learn.

I cannot ignore my daughters' emotions,
in this short but crucial phase of family life.
I won't make light of the provocations, however minor they seem,
or make fun of their sweeping waves of anguish and injustice.
The frustration and fury that knocks them to the floor, even

when I can see that the cause of their agony is disproportionate to their pain.

Rending their clothes because they aren't allowed to watch one more cartoon.

Beating the floor because it's time for bed.

Crushing the gingerbread man to vicious crumbs because his arm had broken off, rendering him inedible.

Our emotions are not private now, each of us is bound tightly to the joys and pains of the others.

Our house becomes a delicate ecosystem, where all happiness is dependent on the actions of the others. One unsettled element, bringing down the rest.

And when I can,

I pause.

And breathe.

Try to remember that they cannot learn control without losing it first.

Try to remember that they don't know, yet, the things I know, that all of it matters, each small battle a loss or victory that will help them in the end.

❀

At weekends we go out into the world together, joining all the other families with their packed lunches and wet wipes, traipsing the children around museums and country parks. Straining for

a better view of dinosaur skeletons or stomping in wellington
boots through the mazes of minor stately homes. In February,
the Maritime Museum hosts a celebration for Chinese New Year,
entrancing the children with dragon dancers and drummers,
teenage volunteers who show them how to make paper rats.
In the main exhibition the girls are thrilled to find a stuffed
emperor penguin exactly their height, standing to attention in a
glass case. They pose for a picture, one either side of it, arms held
stiffly by their sides, chests puffed out. The days out are joyful, but
hard work, even more so now we have to balance the needs of two
energetic four-year-olds and a baby still tethered to nap times.
After lunch we split into teams. Beth takes the older girls to run
around in a ship-themed play area where they climb fake rigging
and swab pretend decks. I take the baby for a walk, keeping the
pushchair moving on the smooth museum floor, rocking her to
sleep under nautical flags and figureheads. From above, I watch
her settle, finding a place to rest her head, tucking her forehead
against the fleecy hood of the pushchair cover. Her eyes close,
small fists holding fast to her teddy, and I look for a quiet corner
of the museum where she can sleep. I steer her into a tiny stand-
alone gallery, a slick black box in the centre of the museum's main
atrium. Inside, it is softly dark, a handful of people standing in
silence, all turned to face the far end of the room, towards the
gallery's one exhibit. Turner's *The Battle of Trafalgar* fills the
whole wall, a huge painting, twelve feet long and eight feet tall.
I push the baby further into the small gallery, gently rocking,
forward a step and back a step, as I read the curator's notes,

printed in white on the black walls.
The height of the battle.
The symbolism of the signalling flags.
The crew of HMS *Victory*,
fighting,
floundering.
And I learn about what came first, Turner's daily notebooks, the
pages and pages of hand-sized sketches he made, searching for a
way to pin all the shadows of the weather onto a piece of paper.
Studies of sky.
The baby sleeps and I look at the painting, each minute
brushstroke that makes up its whole.

screen

Like all the best traditions, the symbolism is obvious.
Posing for a photograph on the front doorstep to mark the first
day of school.
The threshold between home and the outside world.

As is customary, the uniform is slightly too big. A prudent
defence against fast-growing children.
An extra layer of protection against reality. Royal-blue sleeves
dangling past their wrists. Grey skirts over the knee.
A cocoon.
I take the first picture and look at the screen of my phone. So
much about them made clear in a single picture. Our twin
daughters stand, side-by-side, both beaming with excitement
about the big day.
One girl smiling, her hands neatly clasped, her cardigan
buttoned from top to bottom.
The other a blur, jumping up and down on the spot. Every item of
clothing creased and untucked, although she is barely three steps
beyond the house.

The night before, I had laid out their uniforms, placing the
unworn shoes at the ends of their beds, hanging the pleated skirts
on the wardrobe door. Like a wedding, or job interview, a day so
important your clothes need to be ready, waiting up for you all
night. I reach over the top bunk to tuck one girl in.
Kneeling down to the bottom bunk to kiss goodnight to the
other.

—I love you bigger than the whole solar system. She whispers in my ear.

    —How much do you love me?

—The same I say, even bigger. The biggest thing.

Their first day of school marks the end of a summer like no other. Months where the borders of our lives were redrawn. The five of us living, working, playing, eating, exercising, growing, in this house.

    A test.

        A new forging.

—The pandemic is a gift, my friend says, an opportunity to teach
        our children how to see grief, then live through it.
So we built dens with blankets and fairy lights. We made paper dolls and slipped around in our socks on the hall tiles, pretending to be Olympic ice skaters. The children changed into their swimming costumes and splashed together in the bath, pretending it was a pool. It would have been idyllic if it wasn't so frightening.

Like everyone that year we learned to see our friends and family on screens instead. At weekends the children played virtual scavenger hunts with their cousins. They went to online birthday parties and online yoga classes and online playdates. The baby started to hug the phone when my mother called, kissing her face on the screen. And there was connection in it, despite the distances between us. Painting rainbow pictures to display in the windows. Sending postcards covered in hearts and kitten stickers to their friends. My father starts to make handmade stained-glass treasures, sending them to the children through the post in layers of bubble wrap and brown paper. Colourful suncatchers of all their favourite things. A bee. A ladybird. A small blue-glass bird.

And through it all the children asked their small impossible questions. When will it be over? When can we see our friends? When can we go to school?

Soon, we had said.

Soon.

Soon.

A strange autumn has come all the same. Families are told to stretch apart again. A version of normal. Although parents are not allowed to go inside the school gate. Although children must wash their hands in sterilizing soap, playing and learning outside as much as possible. At least they don't know any different, Beth and I say to each other. This is the only version of school they know.

I share the doorstep picture with the family WhatsApp group. Messages buzz back. How smart they look. How grown-up.

A neighbour offers to take a picture of all five of us, so we squash together on the front doorstep. Beth and I stand at the back, the schoolgirls sit on the bottom step, the baby between them,

grinning wildly at this sudden change to the morning routine.
When she hands the phone back to me there are fifty tiny family
portraits on the screen.
—There must be one, she says, where all of you are looking at
the camera.

We go back into the house to collect book bags and the baby's
pushchair. The children hopping and fidgeting in the hallway
with anticipation. All summer we have sold the idea of school.
How exciting it will be, to make new friends, to learn to read
and write. We don't mention all the other lessons they will
learn too, the subtle arts of playground politics, the irritation of
being hemmed in by rules, the heartbreak of wanting to please a
teacher.

As we lock the front door, the baby begins to bounce in the seat
of her pushchair, caught up in the excitement of the morning,
the strangeness of her sisters' new school clothes. With a
final adjustment of shoe buckles and hair slides, we begin the
expedition along our street, past the train station and the corner
shop. The streets full of smiling nervous families, all making the
same journey towards the first day of school.

A parent's job description on the first day of school is clear
enough. We are to conceal any nervousness, projecting only a
sunny confidence about the whole affair. Beth and I might know
that this day marks the beginning of a whole new phase in their

lives but all they need to know is, there will be new toys to play with, and almost certainly something with custard for lunch.

And truly there is no need to feel nervous. I know they are ready. Bright and confident and keen to learn. I know how much they have strained towards this day all through the long lockdown months. But school will surely bring questions from other children, misplaced words from unthinking adults. Attitudes about our family which may hurt their feelings. When they are at school, they will have to speak for us.

At the school gate each family takes their turn to say goodbye. Parents crouch to give final face-to-face instructions. Reminders to tell the teacher if they need the toilet. Reassurances that we will all be here again at the end of the day. A final hug or wipe of the nose before they cross through to the other side. Beth and I kiss the girls on the tops of their heads and straighten their coats. They turn to the gate.
They hold hands,
and walk in.
We wave and wave and wave.

⊛

All that day, as I try to keep my mind on work, I sneak glances at the photos on my phone. Photos of our schoolchildren. Maybe, I tell myself, I'm feeling like this because of the strangeness of the year. How unusual it is to send children into a school that you can't set foot in. Maybe it would always have been this way, each small milestone another jolt.

At lunchtime a friend sends me a black-and-white meme of some schoolchildren sitting behind rows of desks with the caption: 'Congratulations! You've done your shift, they're the teacher's problem now!'
I forward it to Beth with the melodramatic note, 'Our babies are all grown up' and a sad-face emoji.
She replies instantly, and not unreasonably, with:
—They still can't be relied upon to put their knickers on the right way round without advice. Get back to work.

At three o'clock we wrestle the baby back into her pushchair and repeat it all in reverse. The girls skip home, singing alphabet songs and listing all their new friends. A girl with orange hair. A boy who has a dog. We pester them for more news, what was it like, what did you eat at lunch? But they only want to talk about the guinea pigs and the stickers the teacher gave them which smell of strawberry ice cream.

In the evening Beth catches me on my phone, scrolling through the doorstep photos again.
—You can pick three, she says. Then delete the rest.
But I am fascinated by them, this gallery of almost identical photographs. The way they capture a moment of nothingness,

the pause before, not the thing itself. I can't stop thinking about why parents feel compelled to take them. Today's photo, the first of a series not yet made. The same pose each year, each year more child, less door. Pictures to convince me this impossible thing is true. The teenagers I don't know yet, posing reluctantly in front of the same front door. On the edge of another threshold. How will I believe it, without photographic evidence, that such fully formed people had once been these handfuls of curious energy in grey flannel and pigtails? That children grow is both the most remarkable and mundane truth. But their growing isn't really up, it's towards and away. A story of potential and possibilities. It is also far too much for anyone to bear.

What can't be changed must be recorded.

◉

The first weeks pass and the girls settle into the routine of school. There are new lessons for us too, how to navigate the parenting cliques, the unwritten rules about who stands where in the playground. The subtle etiquette of the parents' group chat. As the children form new friendships, bonds between parents grow too. A small boy, all curly hair and space facts, becomes instantly absorbed into the girls' gang. Each morning, the three of them meet on the street corner on the way to school, racing between lampposts, squabbling over whose turn it is to hide behind the bin at the train station. It is remarkable really, how awkward we parents are by comparison. How out of practice we all are

at the business of making friends, so far from the open-hearted
enthusiasm of our children. Instead, we make polite small talk
as we walk behind the children each morning and afternoon.
Taking it in turns to bellow warnings down the street. Wait at
the corner. Remember the road. We talk about the school, our
common ground, and in between share shy details about what we
do for a living, what we're planning to cook for dinner that night.
Civil, cautious steps towards friendship, as our children kiss and
embrace on the street corner, squealing with delight in their daily
group hug. When we prise them apart they call out at the tops of
their voices as they head towards home, goodbye! I'll miss you!
See you tomorrow. Goodbye. Goodbye.

Each day they come home full of new knowledge. The names of
planets, the lifecycle of the frog,
and other important news from the big wide world. A new
understanding of all the small differences that matter.

> Some children speak other languages.
>
> Some parents don't live together.
>
> Some children have everything, they tell us. Puppies.
>
> Televisions in bedrooms.
>
> Some leverage at last,

some bargaining power.

The first weeks pass and we all adapt to what school will be like
this year.
Parents' faces hidden behind masks.
Children handed over one by one in the fresh air,

no joyous collective stream of children as the bell rings.
No friends home for tea.
So much of their new life feels hidden because of it.
Parents' evening is cancelled, school gate chats with the teacher
are discouraged.
Instead, the school gives us a photo app and sends dispatches
directly to my phone.
Emails alert me to new postings and I tap to open them, finding
the children smiling, in the palm of my hand. Small pictures
of the girls drawing maps and building cardboard skeletons.
Climbing and counting and spelling words in play-dough. The
teachers add chirpy captions,
—Today everyone had great fun learning about mammals!
—What a great repeating pattern!
—Super handwriting!
Parents comment back, click to 'like' the posts,
                    small love notes passed between us.

At first I wonder if the app is really necessary; doesn't pausing to
take a picture disrupt the children?
Do we really need to witness all aspects of their lives? But I'm
hungry for the information, the screen of my phone a porthole
into their world, each message a postcard of classroom life. And
why should school be the exception? All of these children are well
used to being photographed, their images preserved and curated
in their parents' phones.
            Chubby faces smeared in the first ice cream.

Videos of first steps.

The first tooth to grow. The first tooth to fall out.

Pictures of the day they were born. Pictures of before they
were born.

I hold them all in the palm of my hand, scrolling backwards and
forward in time.

This day last year.

This day three years ago.

Some are pictures of events that needed marking with a
photograph.

Most are of days when nothing much happened at all.

Days when a camera is all you have to help you pause time.

At half-term we visit my parents and my mum entertains the girls
with old photo albums. She shows them photos from a parallel
universe, another schoolgirl, a different front door. They turn
the pages and touch the photos, printed and protected under
cellophane. But it isn't the size or the quality of the pictures that's
different. It isn't the fact that we're looking at them in a book
not on a screen. These photographs are different because they
are rare. I remember them being taken, all the fuss and effort of
it. The camera dredged up from the back of a sock drawer the
night before. A scurry for film and batteries. It was just more
unusual then, to have your picture taken. People pointed cameras
at children blowing out birthday candles or posing next to a
sandcastle. I don't remember anyone taking a picture of me just
eating my dinner or reading a book. What does it do to them,

this constant recording? Does it make them self-conscious, too aware that they are being looked at? Or is it the opposite, an increased confidence? Turning boldly to the camera each time to pose and smile. What does it do to us? This compulsion to keep photographing them. Distracting us from living in the present. Scrolling back through the images, the proof that we are all of these people, all at once.

And we are strict about this, or so we like to think, never letting a child play with a phone in a restaurant. Only putting cartoons on in the car for the longest journeys. Still, when the baby tries to wake me, she points to my glasses and phone on the bedside table, urging me to take up the two essential extensions to my body, telling me to start my day,
to start looking,
seeing.

Sometimes the children ask to borrow my phone to send messages.
Rows and rows of small emojis for their favourite aunt.
Each icon carefully chosen to convey just the right meaning.
—A red heart, because I love her.
—A mermaid, because she's beautiful.
—A pizza slice, because I'm hungry.

Sometimes, I leave my phone on the kitchen table, then find it again later, one hundred and seventy-five pictures of a Lego

small

castle. Sixty-two selfies, all eyes and fringe. When the older two
play with the phone together they make shows, dressing up and
making videos, pulling faces and dancing.
—Let me see. Let me see.
Another way of looking at themselves.
The same thing, I think, as when I find one of them,

alone,

standing in front of the mirror.

Working something out.

◉

By November it seems as if they have always gone to school.
The routines and rituals of it are so embedded in our lives.
By November they have already changed,
newly alert to the world,
sensitive to other people, the things they say and think.
Each day that winter term we walk home in a straggling group
with other children from their class. Parents catching trailing
coats and bags. Dogs on leads. Younger siblings in pushchairs.
All the chaotic chatter of the day between us.
On the afternoon my daughter trips, she doesn't cry,
she isn't hurt.

Instead, she blushes.

For the first time.
She looks at her friends to see who has noticed and buries her red
face in the sleeve of my coat. So I cover for her, a human shield

until the blush fades. As we walk on, she presses tightly against my side and when we both see that nobody is looking, I bend down to whisper in her ear,

—Don't worry, I tell her. There's no shame in falling.

girls

They ask about her all the time,
the small girl I used to be.
The things she liked and did.

I watch my oldest daughters not in awe now, but recognition.
Babies and toddlers live in a place you know you have visited,
but can't truly recall. Something crucial about them remains
mysterious. But at four, then five years old, the girls become
recognizable in a new way, revealing all the small things we have
in common.

How little any of us can tolerate losing at board games.
How hard we try to conceal that fact.
How happy we all are in the company of colouring pencils
or books.

Small coincidences. Shared passions that bind us.

I watch the two of them, playing side-by-side, lost for hours at
the kitchen table. As they build new worlds from shoe boxes
and sticky tape, I remember my own long-forgotten projects.
Scientific experiments conducted at the bathroom sink with
shampoo and shaving foam. A months-long obsession with an
illustrated first-aid manual. Crucial investigations. They don't
need me to interfere, to witness. So much growing and making
sense of the world happens in hours like this. The small spaces
in between, staring out of the window on a long car journey,
looking at the patterns on the curtain before you fall asleep. I
recognize it and I admire it, the unrelenting busyness of small

girls. The strength of their focus. Small girls, like all of us, need time to think.

But there's something else too, a reminder of my betrayal.

Didn't I, didn't we all, swear an oath that we would be different?

Didn't we promise that we would grow into adults who would always let children jump on the sofa?

Vow that we would let chocolate run from the very taps.

But here I am, handing out the same old orders,

> telling small girls what to do,
>
> what to eat,
>
> when to sleep.

The benevolent constraints placed on loved children.

Because it is unbelievable.

That we were once so much like them.

That they will become much more like us.

The more they ask me about her, the more I remember. The memory of living in a girl's body, quick and fluid. The itchiness of carpeted bus seats on the backs of your thighs. The questions you couldn't ask. Secrets you couldn't tell. I tell them now, to my sympathetic confessors. The frogspawn I stole from the neighbour's pond. The paint I chipped on the radiator and covered up with white correction fluid. The stories of girlhood that make me exist to them in new ways. Of being a girl, just like them. Fallible and worried and bold.

I know that the freedoms of girlhood are too short-lived.

Keep running, I want to tell them, as fast as you can. Take up all the space you need, sing all day if you want to. Revel in the perfection of your small body, don't apologize for it. Don't fear it. You are absolutely right. Low brick walls are to be walked on, not beside. Tables are indeed structures to be approached on or under. Small girls know all the benefits of their size, the freedoms and possibilities of a small body. The pleasure of sitting inside a wardrobe, knees tucked to chin, the smell of shoes and dry cleaning. The thrill of hiding under the bed, a small body held flat against the carpet, or being posted through the small kitchen window when the key is locked on the inside. A useful purposeful thing.

A small body can hide in plain sight,

invisible at the top of the stairs, straining to overhear the mumble of adult conversation.

And sometimes I watch them in solidarity, a former girl who knows skill when she sees it.

> The way they dangle from the top of the bunk bed ladder with such panache.

> The bold backflip from the moving roundabout.

She would have applauded it all.

But I didn't know then, what now would feel like.

The burden of foresight that makes me say,

> Don't fall.

> > Be careful.

> > > > Climb down.

small

Because I see, and I remember, how complicated it can be.
A small girl's body is never quite her own.
Even those who protect and care for it take advantage of their power,
tickling it and lifting up.
Moving the body from one place to another.
Controlling, however softly.
I watch them learn hard lessons.
The conventions and expectations that surround them.
Unwritten rules about what small girls' bodies can or should do.
I remember then the strange conversations at the antenatal class,
the ideas about our unborn sons and daughters that had seemed
from another time. The consensus in the room that night that
raising girls required some extra thing, a vigilance, the rallying of
extra parental security.

> Hold hands,
> stay close,
> don't wander off.

The same bogeyman passed on from mother to daughter.
The same advice.

Be on guard.

And they understand, implicitly, the need for girls to hold two
competing thoughts at the same time.
They know that girls can be doctors, astronauts, artists.
All the things their feminist picture books tell them.
They know, too, that some toys, some colours, some ways of

being, are meant for girls, for reasons they could never explain.
The propaganda of girlhood.
They are surrounded by empowering, unapologetic messages:
girls can be anything at all.
And they are seeped, all the same, in the same old stories.
The small whispered reminders that girls' things are less-than
and insignificant.

Girly.

In a house full of girls I can see the obvious truth,
girly things are imagination

and risk

and will

and bravery.

And when they rail against it, when they scream that life is
unfair, that nobody ever listens,
I remember that too.
How much of being a small girl is learning how to digest rage.
The daily frustrations of being talked over, patronized,
underestimated.

◉

The baby doesn't worry about any of this,

yet.

All her years of girlhood stretching out ahead of her.

small

On my first week of parental leave I take her to the baby group in the village community hall. I sit on the mat, wise and battle-worn, among the first-time mothers, their babies neatly pressed for the outing. In their company I see all the things I have learned, all the things they will learn too, in the coming months and years. The practical exams in teething and potty training, the new-found certainty that parenting is nothing more than responding to the things you didn't expect, in the best way you can manage. And there is a novelty to it this time, the convenience of carrying just one baby around. How easily her narrow pram can be manoeuvred into shops. The way we can sit alone together, at small cafe tables. The treat of being in her company. The intimacy of it. But there is something unexpected too, the intensity of caring for just one baby, no third party to distract or diffuse the mood. The reliance we have on one another. Just the two of us, out in the world alone. If the first time round was a miracle, this is a gift not to be squandered. It concentrates the mind, the certain knowledge that you won't get the chance to be a mother again. So I urge myself to remember it all. The nothing weight of her as I lift her from her highchair. The way her presence fills the house, even as she sleeps. I look closely for each small change. The moment she takes on a new gesture, clenching and unclenching her fists to say, 'pick me up' or 'pass me that', calling the things and people she needs to her without words. I spend my days with her looking at the world through a strange kind of vision. Focused intently on trying to absorb the experience, preserving it as it happens. And at the same time, trying to do the opposite. Urging myself to live in the moment. Be here with her now. It is already nearly over.

I commit, once again, to filling the baby's social calendar, signing up to weekly swimming lessons at the local leisure centre. There is something surreal about the lessons, in which a middle-aged man directs a group of women to circle him for an hour, singing nursery rhymes and dunking their babies underwater. Sometimes the babies are thrilled to be in the pool, sometimes they are outraged. Mostly they are bemused by the sounds and colours and smells of it all. They'll sleep well this afternoon, we all say, smugly, to each other as we disperse in the changing rooms each week. Because this, after all, is the whole point of the exercise. One of the swimming lessons falls on Remembrance Day. While we're all in the water the leisure centre tannoy starts to play the 'Last Post', announcing the start of the two minutes' silence. On the far side of the pool, the serious swimmers pause in their lanes, removing their rubber hats and goggles as a mark of respect. In the shallow end, the mums stop singing, and hold our squirming babies as still as we can. Our shushing echoing off the tiles and glass. Afterwards, I walk home so the baby can sleep in the pushchair. Wrapped up in her fleecy cocoon, happy and worn out. The smell of chlorine and rice cakes. I place the back of my hand against her red cheeks just to check, warm enough, but not too warm. I wonder what it is like to sleep like this. Moving. Dreams of flying as we skim along pavements. Bumping over

kerbs and cobblestones to dreams of ships at sea. When we are
halfway home it starts to rain so I take shelter in a tourist cafe. I
buy an overpriced sandwich so I can sit there long enough to wait
out the weather, long enough to let the baby sleep. From my seat
in the window I can see the row of flattened boxes and sleeping
bags, the nests of homeless people who sleep in the shadow of the
castle. They balance their treasures on the deep windowsills of
the bank, a collection of lost toys, dropped from prams by small
hands, or left behind on park benches. A floppy-headed panda, a
grubby mouse in a ballerina skirt. Everything is getting soaked.
The rain stops so I pay, racing to finish our walk home before she
wakes up. The river runs fast with the rain now, the water high
and grey. As I push my sleeping baby over the bridge I feel a sort
of vertigo, a flashing premonition that the water will leap up and
swallow her. For a moment I'm sure that this baby, who cannot
walk, will leap from her pushchair into the river. I grip the handle
tighter, push her to the other side.
Because sometimes it is like this.

This love that looks like fear.
Sometimes, I can hear them, cracking their skulls on the stairs.
Sometimes I can see them, falling from the branch,
or stepping off the kerb,
or slipping from my grasp.
Because this is motherhood too.
All your smallest worries magnified. Everything far too close.

I don't go to the swimming classes to teach the baby to swim.

I go to spend half an hour in the company of other women who are worried their baby might drown.

Mothers find each other, in the places mothers go to while their husbands are somewhere else. Somewhere in the real world, doing real things. And often the mothers will ask me about him, my putative husband, if he is good with the baby, if he helps after work. Because the baby on my lap shapes the world around me into a singular story. What I am like. Who I love. And they ask me all the compulsory questions, how old the baby is, if I have others. As we stand, side-by-side, pushing the swings. Like the woman with the same coat as me, my double, who had said,
—Your poor husband, talk about outnumbered. A houseful
of women!
And I had said.
—She doesn't mind,
And we pushed the swings. Side-by-side.

But sometimes, do I dare admit it? Sometimes, I just smile, let the assumption wash over me in chlorinated waves. I dunk the baby, or push the swing, or sip the tea, and say

nothing.
Sometimes I am just too tired. Sometimes it is cowardice, a shameful avoidance of awkwardness or confrontation, because I have had this conversation enough times now to know that the outcomes are unpredictable. That the correction might lead to a polite apology, a tiny readjustment of one person's worldview

quietly flashing across their face. Or it might be something else. Something worse or something more enthusiastic. The reassurances from a stranger that her cousin is gay, actually, and one of her friends at college was too, for a while. And if I don't say something to the stranger mothers, if I don't correct, or edit, or insert the word wife into the conversation,

there is always a price to pay.

Guilt.

The conversation playing on loop.

All the chances missed to be brave.

To be truthful.

®

Days at home with the baby are dominated by all the domestic fluster caused by the other two. I set her on the kitchen floor with a drum kit of saucepans and wooden spoons as I work through the endless washing and folding of their small clothes. The daily deadline of making sure the spaghetti Bolognese is ready for when her sisters come home in the afternoon, hungry and full of stories. I feel it more keenly this time, the absence of the things which usually define me, the clothes and places that feel mine. It is impossible not to be changed by this shift from work to home, a turn away from all other responsibilities, pulled instead to meet the needs of this small person. This small person who has changed the dynamics of our family, tested our limitations. And it's as it should be, for now. The baby is not interested in the

nuance of my personality, she does not care about my views or
ambitions. All she expects is that I be everything she needs.
And I do it, give myself over to her. Bend to her will.
I resolve not to hold back, embracing this stage of motherhood
which I won't see again. I start wearing mum drag, high-waisted
jeans and headscarves knotted in my hair. I throw myself into
the deepest of clichés, sitting with the other mums at the edge of
the sports hall, while the older children chase a football in and
out of cones. Chatting about whether the baby slept last night.
Comparing notes on who has remembered to buy the ingredients
for pancake day.

And I'd be a liar to pretend I don't see the privilege of it, the
way people speak to me when I am dressed like this, when I am
holding a baby or pushing a pram. How they tell me things or
trust me, with a bag or a secret, just like that. I wonder what
people see when they do this. Someone unthreatening. Some
collective evidence of humanity ticking over in the image of a
woman wiping a toddler's sticky chin. And sometimes, when it
happens, I have the feeling that I have fooled them. That I am
impersonating someone else, moving and acting in the ways a
mother is supposed to.
And is it such a betrayal? To be drawn to the soft landing of
conventionality?
To break the rules of motherhood, sometimes.
To play along at others.
Maybe I do it because it makes me feel closer to my own mother,

small

because it makes me feel as though I am her.

Because of course I lost her for a while, in the usual ways. Pulling
out of her orbit when I was a teenager, because that happens.
A little further when I went to university, because that's normal.
A bit more again when I told her I was gay, because that happens
too.

Because she had been sure, then, that this and that were opposite
things.
My coming out an end to my motherhood long before it began.
An instead life, not an also.
And now I watch her, reading my daughters the stories of her
own girlhood. Magical lands at the tops of trees, smugglers,
adventures, ginger beer picnics. The girls sit, either side of her, one
chewing a strand of hair, the other frowning in concentration.
I listen to them talking as I make their beds. Their endless
questions about the book, grilling my mother for explanations,
for more details. Her patience.
A circle completing itself.
Like watching myself.
Then and now
and in time to come.
She is a key to me and they know it. Your mother's mother is the
holder of all secrets.
—Tell us again, they say, about when Mummy was a little girl.
        When you were.

And she tells them, stories of other mothers, other daughters, in her house of small treasures, chocolate biscuits and barely used felt pens. The Russian dolls she takes down from the shelf when we visit so the girls can arrange them in a neat parade. Grandmother, mother, daughter. Fighting over who gets to hold the smallest doll, a tiny wooden skittle of a baby at the centre of them all.

That evening I catch a glimpse of them together. My mother in the armchair by the window, my baby on her lap, warm and soft from her bath, looking her in the eye to say out loud, —you are so loved.

A seed, firmly planted, to grow there forever.

●

In the darkness of our bedroom, early morning light leaks through the shutters. The baby is flat on her back between us, holding her doll in the air, tending to its needs. She opens and closes the Velcro on its clothes, smooths its non-existent hair, sets it down on the pillow. Then she takes it up again and squeezes it to her chest. When the doll is asleep, she turns to me. Patting my head and poking her fingers in my eyes to keep them closed. She tucks the covers around my neck and kisses me, loudly. Mothering in all the ways she knows. I scoop her up and carry her to the kitchen. It's her first birthday and there is work to be done. By lunchtime, the house is full of people, the baby overwhelmed

with wooden puzzles and books that make farm animal noises.
Her sisters generously help her to blow out her single candle
and she spreads great fistfuls of chocolate cake across her face.
As everyone marvels at the impossibility that a whole year has
passed, she crawls between us all, muscling into conversations.
—Me. she implores, reaching up to be lifted.
—Me? when she wants a share of someone else's lunch.
—Me! to be noticed, and included.
—Me, ME. all day long, to be seen. To be heard.

Afterwards, Beth and I tidy up the party mess and talk about our
final baby, hardly a baby at all now. How much she wants to stand
on her own two feet, in all ways possible. We look over and see
her, pulling herself up to stand against the sofa.

Beth takes the birthday girl up for her bath and I seek out the
others. I find them, sitting together, deep in a typical conversation.
—Do you know Annabel?
—Yeah
—She got struck by lightning in a storm and had to go
        to hospital.
—That's a fib, she did that on her mummy's hair straighteners.
—It's true, I've seen the scar and touched it with my finger.
And it is hard not to miss being a girl at times like this, how much
fun it would be to jump into this conversation.
What a gift it is, anyway, to hear them, to be close.

Isn't this, in the end, how families work? Each of us caught up in tangles of ourselves.

Pasts and presents all at once. Memories of who we have been, small clues that hint at who we might become. I think of him on their birthdays, a prayer of thanks as they blow out their candles. The small gift that made this whole world possible.

On Monday real life begins again; the baby will start nursery, I'll go back to work. I'll stand on the doorstep in unfamiliar clothes and hand her over, her little bag packed with her teddy and spare socks. I'll smile and wave goodbye. I'll ignore her eyes saying, don't leave me here, her arms reaching out. The unspoken betrayal, I thought you felt the same as me, I thought you understood we are one. Then I'll sit for a few moments in my car trying not to be a cliché.

Beth calls the girls up for bedtime and I go back to the kitchen to finish the party washing-up. Through the baby monitor I hear it, the sound of Beth teaching our daughters to read. Sitting side-by-side on the bedroom floor

     breaking words into sounds

          before piecing them back into sentences.

     Building stories,

            word

   by

               word.

epilogue

A note for my daughters

I wrote this book in the small moments in between. On hospital chairs between your incubators. I wrote some parts before you woke up and some in the middle of the night as you slept. I wrote a good deal of it while Mama bore all the weight of dinner and bath time so I could make some progress. I wrote it, of course, for you.

Mothers and daughters have a bond of steel rope, strong and lasting but sore if you grip it too tightly. Sometimes I am too busy to play. Sometimes I am tired. Sometimes I am frustrated that you want to be lifted up and held against my shoulder at 4am. I try to remember that, soon enough, I won't be able to lift you, and worse, that you won't want me to.

We have already been so many different people to each other. A family that has made and remade itself several times over. Everything will be different again by the time you are old enough to read this. By then you will have stopped looking at me in the way you do now. You will have stopped running towards me whenever I come into a room. You will have stopped believing in me so steadfastly. You will be angry with me sometimes, embarrassed by my clothes, disappointed in my decision-making. And I will feel the same about you every now and again. For now, our disagreements are mostly minor health and safety disputes. Battles of will. Boundaries set and tested. We'll find new things to argue about when you're not five and two years old I'm sure.

small

There are stories in this book about me and Mama before you were born, although I can hardly believe that such people existed. Stories about the years when I could not imagine you, and the years when I could think of nothing else. There are stories about the very first people you were and the people you had started to become when I was writing about us all. When I watch you now I wonder which parts of you are fixed. Which parts will change.

I have written and rewritten these stories so many times now. The stories of what happened, the stories of why it matters. I have tried to find ways to remember all the small moments that have made us. All the small things you have shown me. I have tried to find the right words to describe what it is like to be your mother. Your mothers.

It is snowing today, but not settling, and the metaphor is all too obvious. I can hear the three of you downstairs, building a castle and a crocodile from egg boxes, sending Mama running for 'More glue! More glue!'

Never stop sticking together.

February 2021

acknowledgements

I am tempted to say that many people have mothered this book into the world. I'm grateful for the chance to thank them all here.

Thank you to my editor, Romilly Morgan, who had faith, in it and me, from the beginning. I'm so glad you could see that what it needed was to be just a little bit more brazen. It's a privilege to be part of such a list.

Thank you to all those at Octopus who took such good care of this book as it took shape, particularly Pauline Bache, Sally Somers, Jonathan Christie, Sarah Kyle, Serena Savini, Hazel O'Brien and Charlotte Sanders.

Enormous thanks are due to my agent, Emma Finn at C&W, who found the book when it was far smaller than this and saw what it could grow into. Thanks also go to Spread the Word for setting the challenge that got it going in the first place, and to Bernardine Evaristo for not letting me stop there.

I'm very grateful to all those who have read drafts along the way and given me the courage to write more. To Helen Cullen, who is an oracle, and to Wayne Holloway-Smith, who understood the importance of a dead mouse. Thanks go to Ellie Roderick for checking I knew my scalpel from my Satinsky Scissors and to Emilie Pine for seeing the value of prophetic plums.

Writing about the family I have made has reminded me how grateful I am for the family who made me. Thank you to my parents for sitting with me while I learned to sleep. Thank you for letting me read and read. A special note of thanks to my nan, who did not help me write this book, but will show it to every person in Wales.

A line of thanks seems too meagre for the many unnamed medics in this book, but here it is all the same. Thank you to the skilled and compassionate men and women of the National Health Service. So much of what I have described here is a tribute to them.

It is surely clear enough that there are four people owed the greatest debt of thanks here. To Bethan, of course. Thank you for letting me tell our story, thank you for reading it over and over again, and thank you for taking the children on a tour of every playground in the county so I could have Saturday mornings to work in peace. You can definitely have the paddle board now. Finally, my biggest thank you is saved for my best girls. Thank you for always asking me how the book was going. Thank you for sharing all your excellent story ideas with me, and thank you for making such good use out of my drafts with your epic paper snowball fights. To Megan Hope, Orla Grace, and Wren Joy, you have, as always, lived up to your names.

Claire Lynch is a university lecturer, academic and critic. Claire's *Four Thought* talk 'The Other Mother' was first broadcast on BBC Radio Four this year and her first piece of narrative non-fiction took second place in the Spread the Word Life Writing Prize in 2017. She was a shortlisted writer on the Penguin Random House WriteNow scheme in 2018 and longlisted for the Hinterland non-fiction Prize in 2019. *small* is her first book for a general audience.

This **brazen** book was created by

Editorial Director: Romilly Morgan
Senior Editor: Pauline Bache
Assistant Editor: Sarah Kyle
Design Director: Jonathan Christie
Cover Designer: Daniel Benneworth-Gray
Copyeditor: Sally Somers
Typesetter: Jonathan Christie
Senior Production Manager: Peter Hunt
Sales: Kevin Hawkins & Dominic Smith
Publicity & Marketing: Hazel O'Brien & Charlotte Sanders
Legal: Imogen Plouviez & Kirsty Howarth